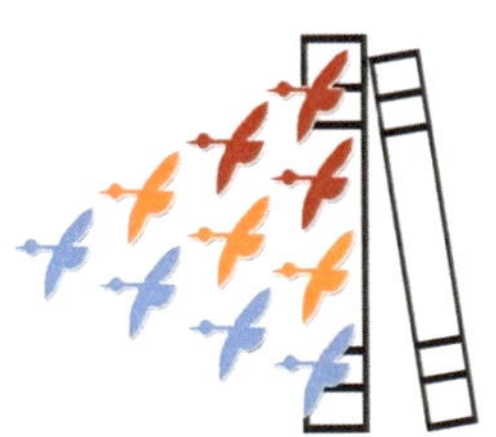

BY **JOSEPH OLSEN**

POETRY

Snapshots
24 Hours
Between Us & Imagination

FOR CHILDREN

Do You Smell That?
Max Finds A Master
A Penny For Dinner:
And Other Children's Poems
For Children And Childish Adults

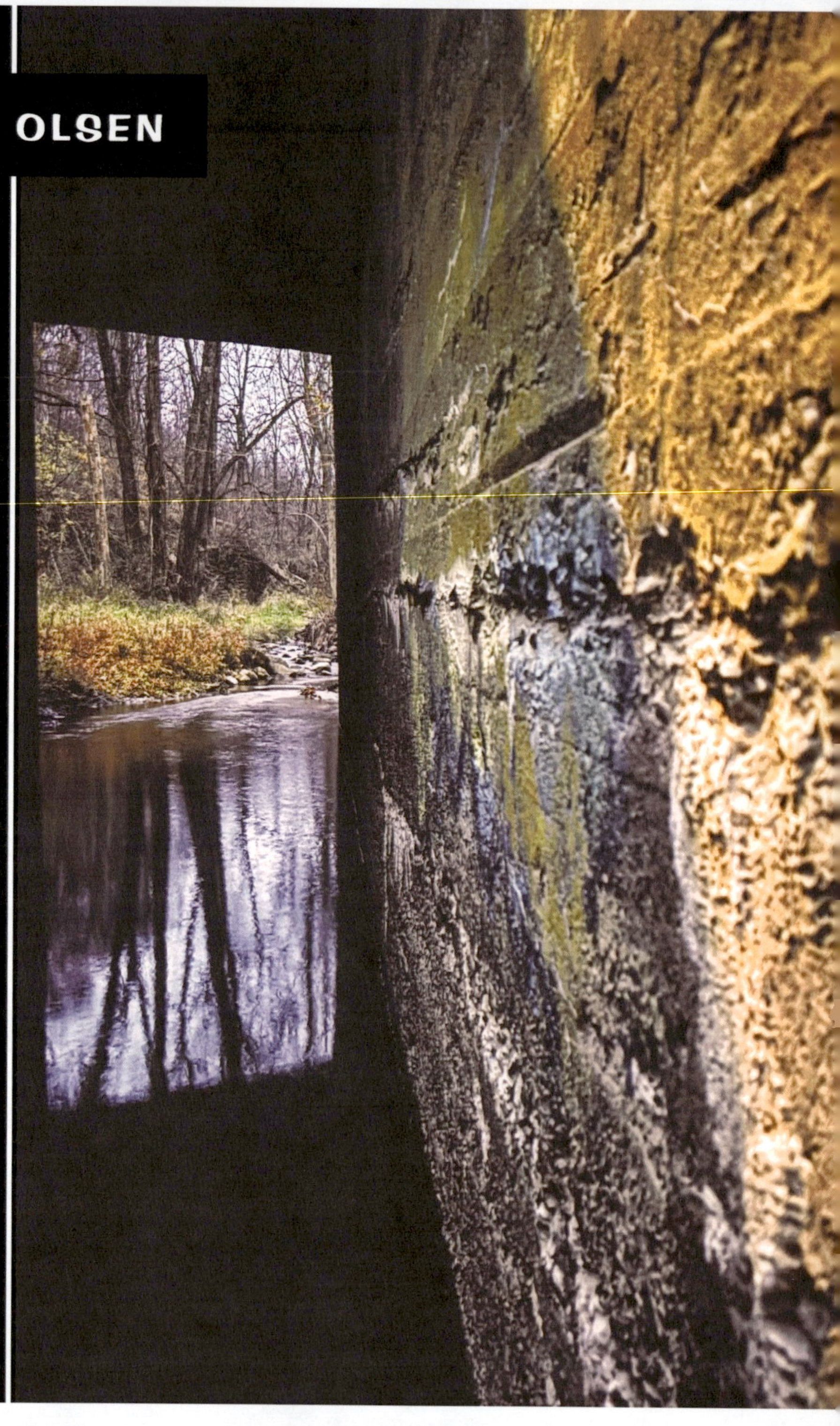

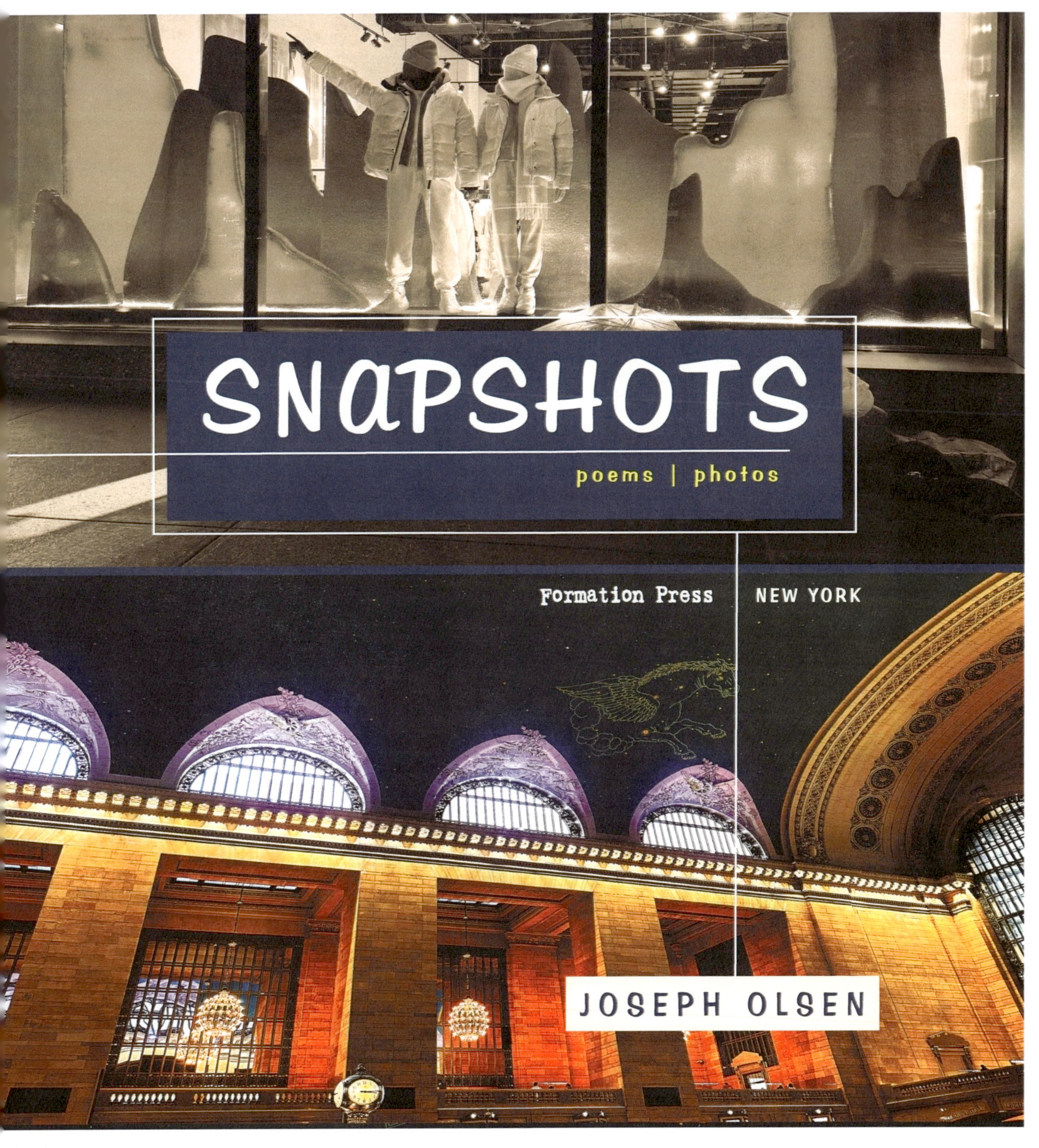

SNAPSHOTS
poems | photos
Formation Press   NEW YORK
JOSEPH OLSEN

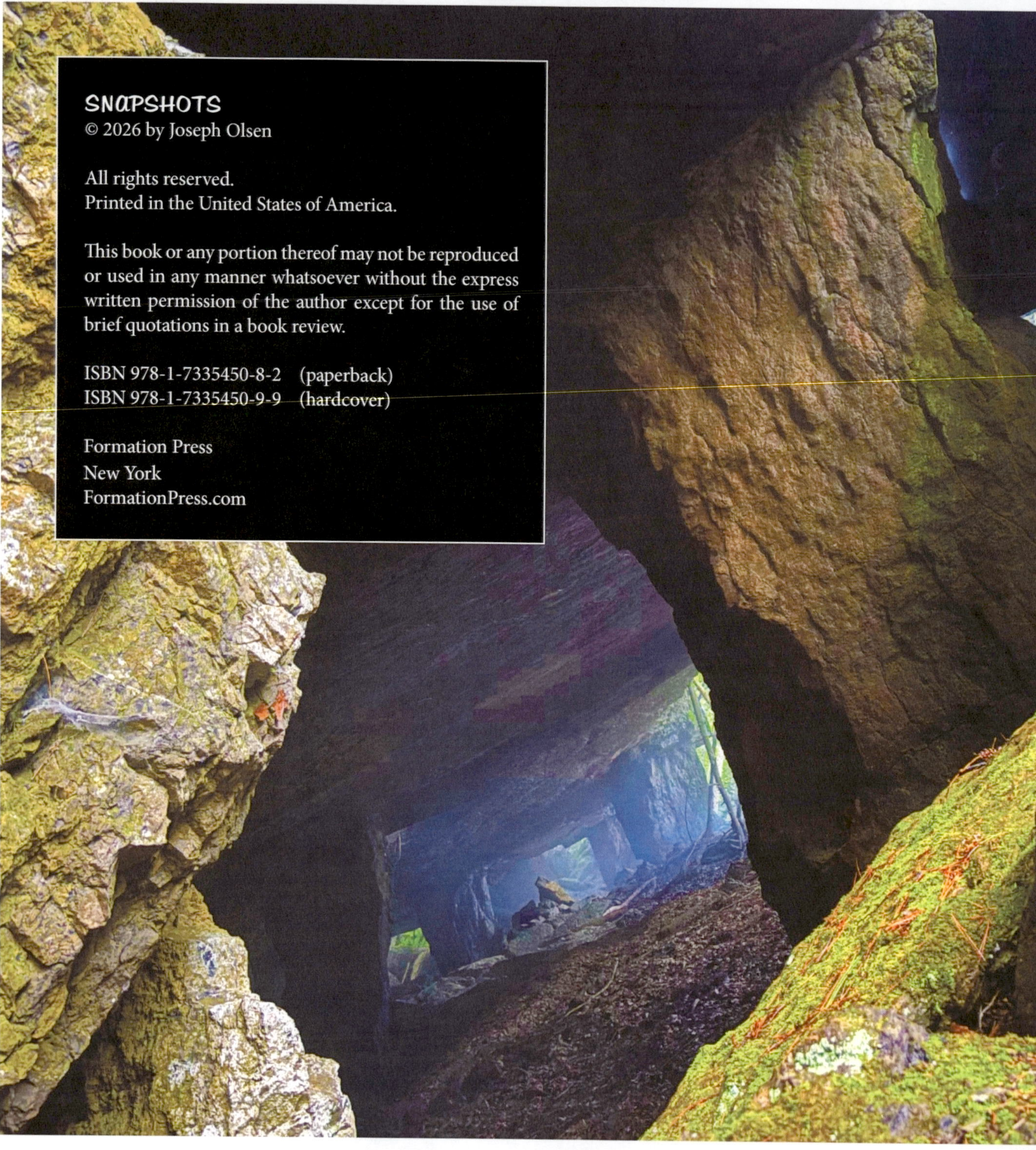

ISBN 978-1-7335450-8-2   (paperback)
ISBN 978-1-7335450-9-9   (hardcover)

Formation Press
New York
FormationPress.com

MY **WIFE** has brought great beauty into my life. And my daughter has brought me nothing but joy. Those qualities were greatly lacking.

-Christopher Meloni

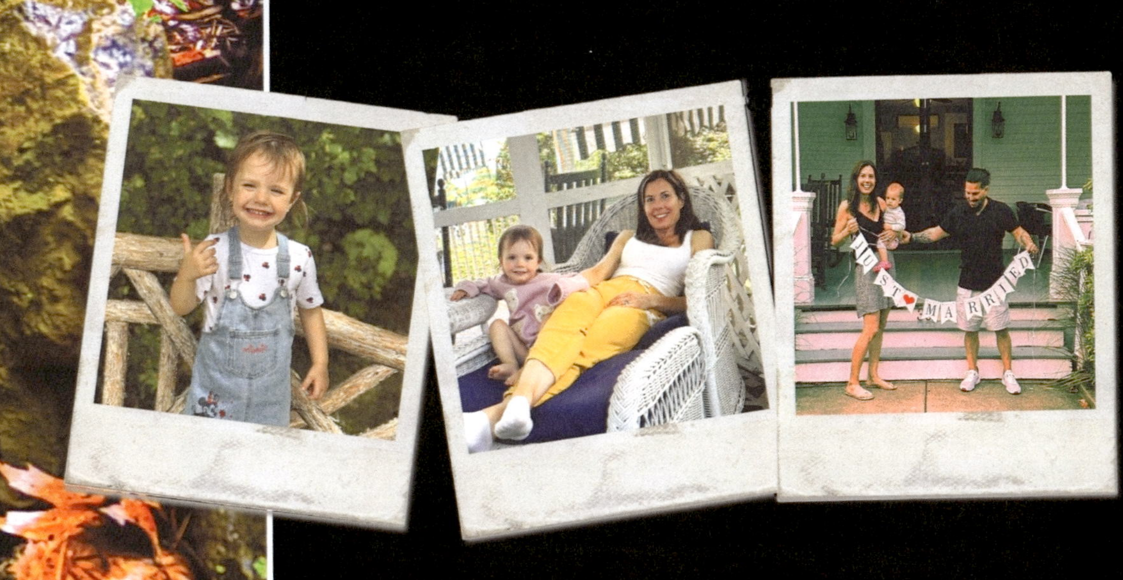

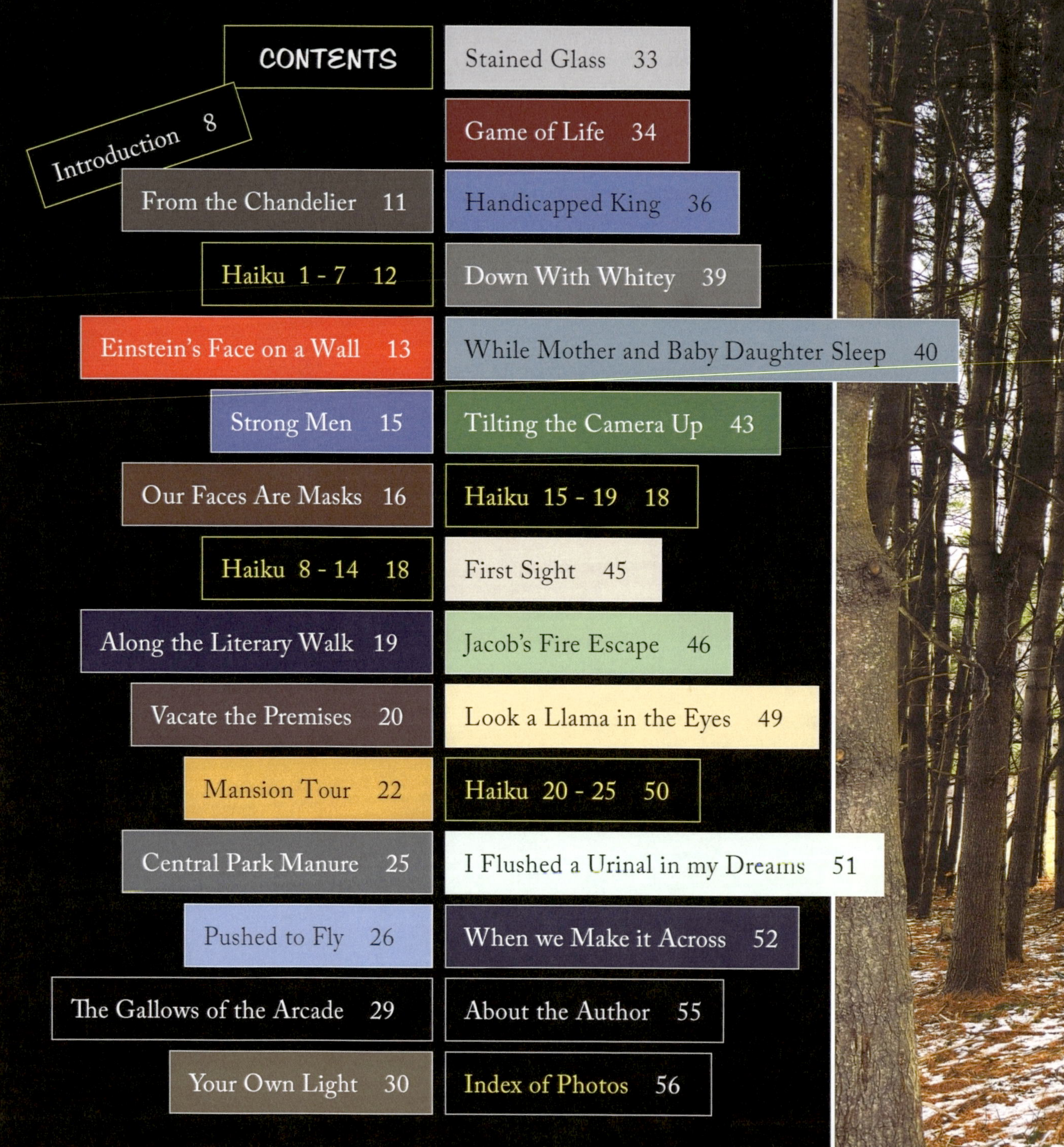

CONTENTS

Introduction 8

From the Chandelier 11

Haiku 1 - 7 12

Einstein's Face on a Wall 13

Strong Men 15

Our Faces Are Masks 16

Haiku 8 - 14 18

Along the Literary Walk 19

Vacate the Premises 20

Mansion Tour 22

Central Park Manure 25

Pushed to Fly 26

The Gallows of the Arcade 29

Your Own Light 30

Stained Glass 33

Game of Life 34

Handicapped King 36

Down With Whitey 39

While Mother and Baby Daughter Sleep 40

Tilting the Camera Up 43

Haiku 15 - 19 18

First Sight 45

Jacob's Fire Escape 46

Look a Llama in the Eyes 49

Haiku 20 - 25 50

I Flushed a Urinal in my Dreams 51

When we Make it Across 52

About the Author 55

Index of Photos 56

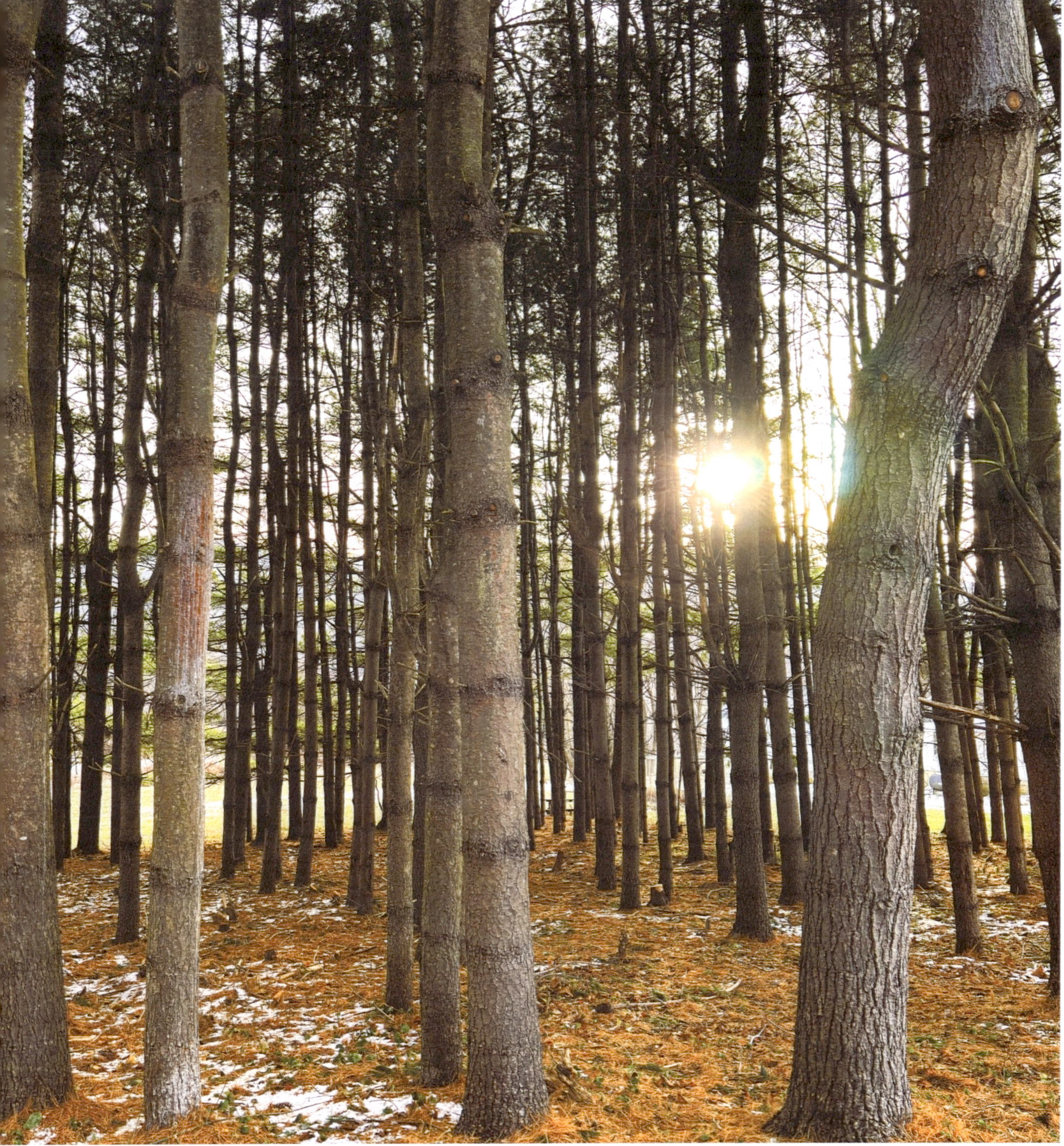

BACK IN 2023,

I grew tired of being an InstaPoet, becoming a product instead of a creator, an influencer instead of a writer. No longer confined to daily posts that begged algorithms for crumbs of attention, I denounced social media all together, sending poems against the background of images found online to the only person in my life worth posting to: my wife. Snapshotting them on her phone, she surprised me one day with a collection from Shutterfly, prompting a collection of my own for publication.

This book, similar to how a photograph freezes a fleeting instant, is a snapshot of my perspective, thoughts and observations through free-verse and haiku against the backdrop of images taken during outings and hikes with my family.

I hope you enjoy every poem and snapshot.

Joseph Olsen
Hudson Valley, NY
January 2026

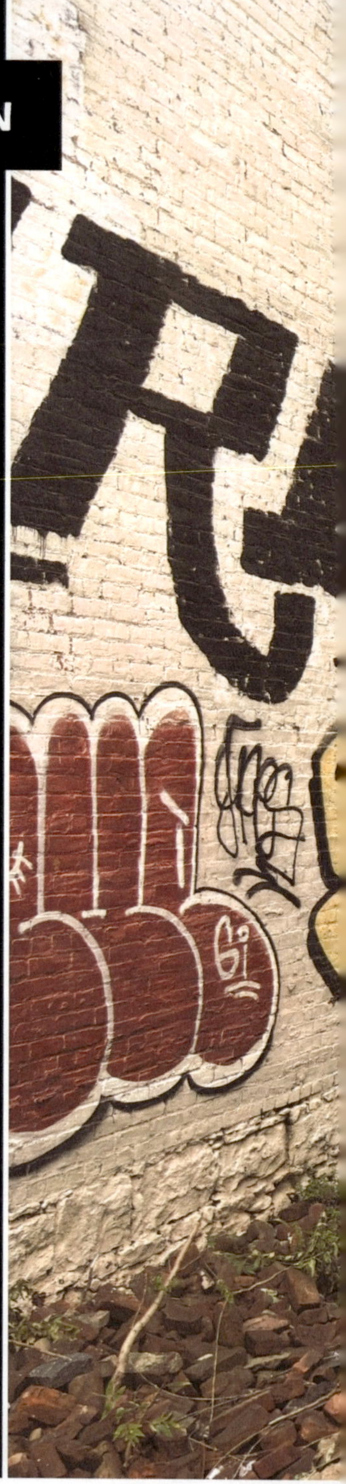

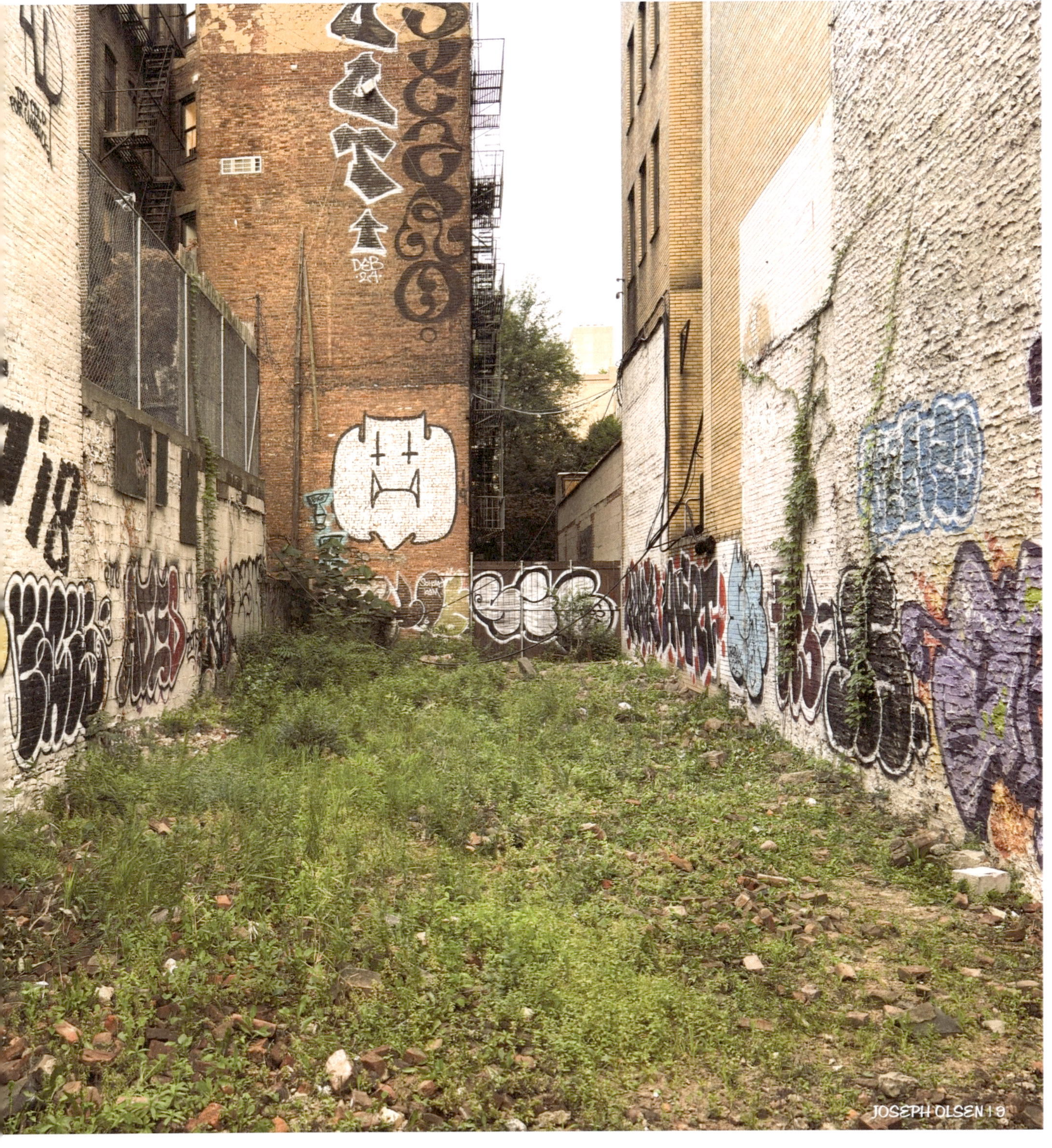
JOSEPH OLSEN 19

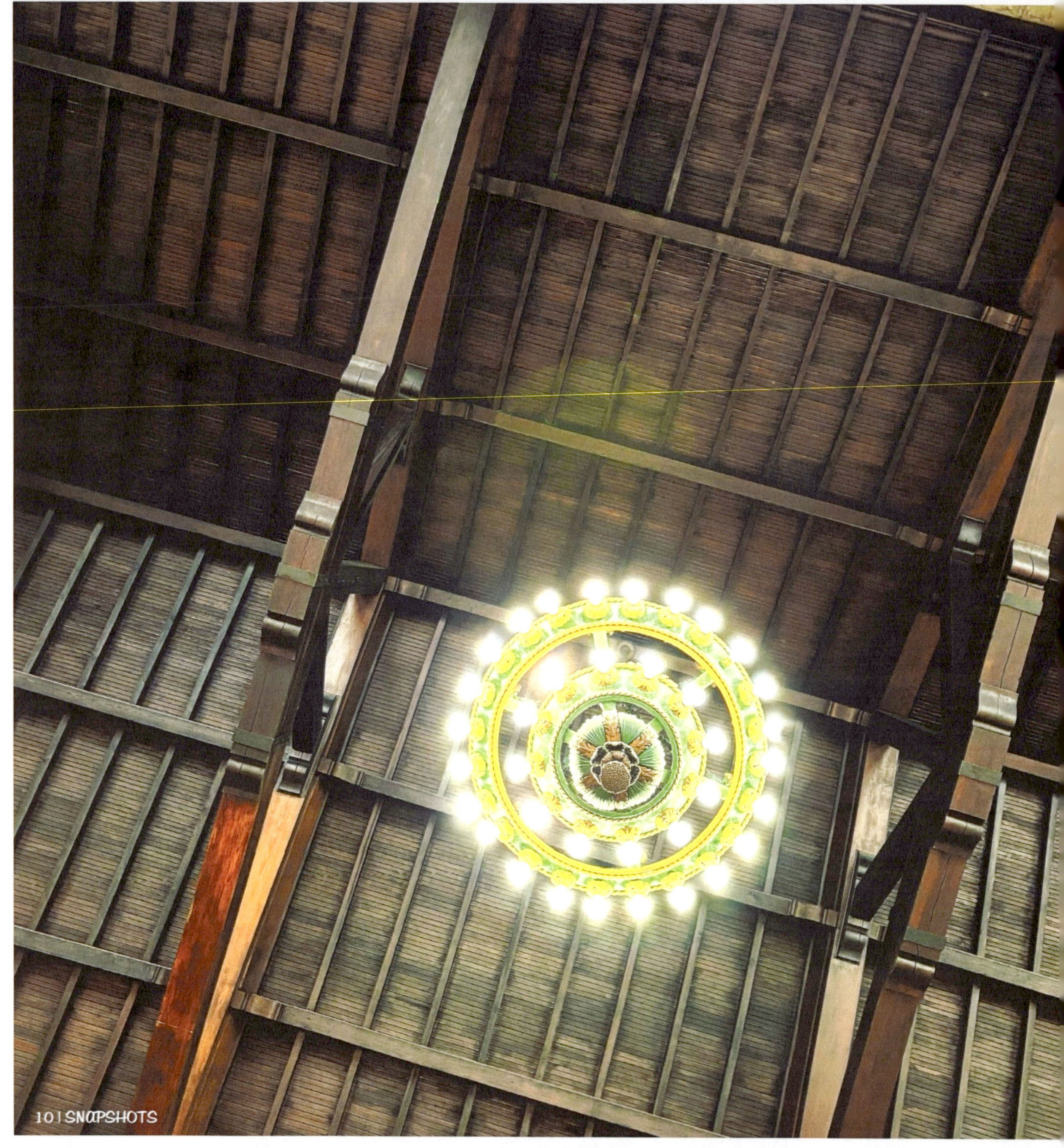

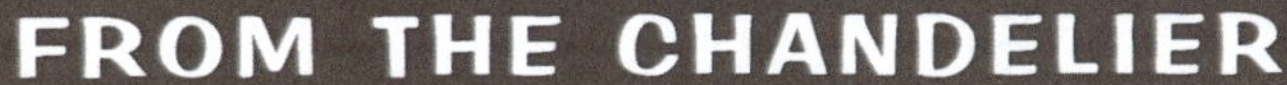

FROM THE CHANDELIER

Somebody has to act a fool
    Track mud into the living room
    Cast the sly shadow of a new moon

Somebody has to be the victim
    Lose more than win
    Mourn the death of kin

Somebody has to criticize assertively
    Trigger fear, threaten the soul
    Test the limits of control

Somebody has to swing from the chandelier
    Oscillate between doubt and desire
    Eventually, come crashing down
    Into a million shimmering pieces

HAIKU 1 - 7

1.

A surreal conversation
A dreamlike midnight
A whimsical rush of love

2.

Disheartened by
The last of
Today's light

3.

Looking back to our birth
Forward to our demise
They Stood Up For Love, Song by Live

4.

Peering at the moon
With pale countenance
A twinkling star

5.

Listening to birdsong
Grow blades
Of grass

6.

Neglecting deeper
Spiritual growth
Low-hanging fruit

7.

When the hymn is done
The empty pews
Adore silence

EINSTEIN'S FACE ON A WALL

Only changed from
One form to another
    As stated
Energy cannot be created
Or destroyed
You remind me
From your spray-painted face
On a wall

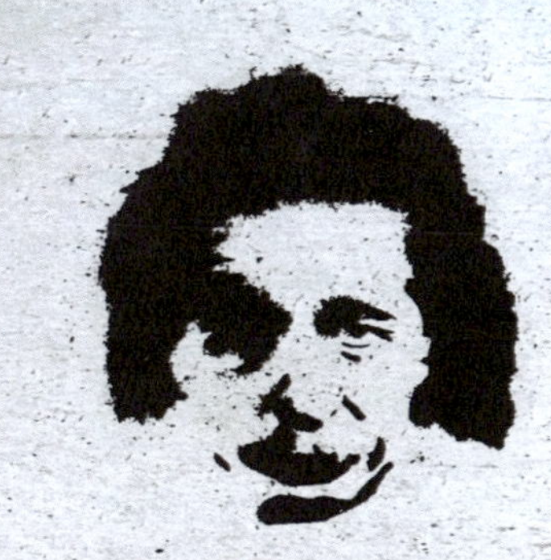

JOSEPH OLSEN | 13

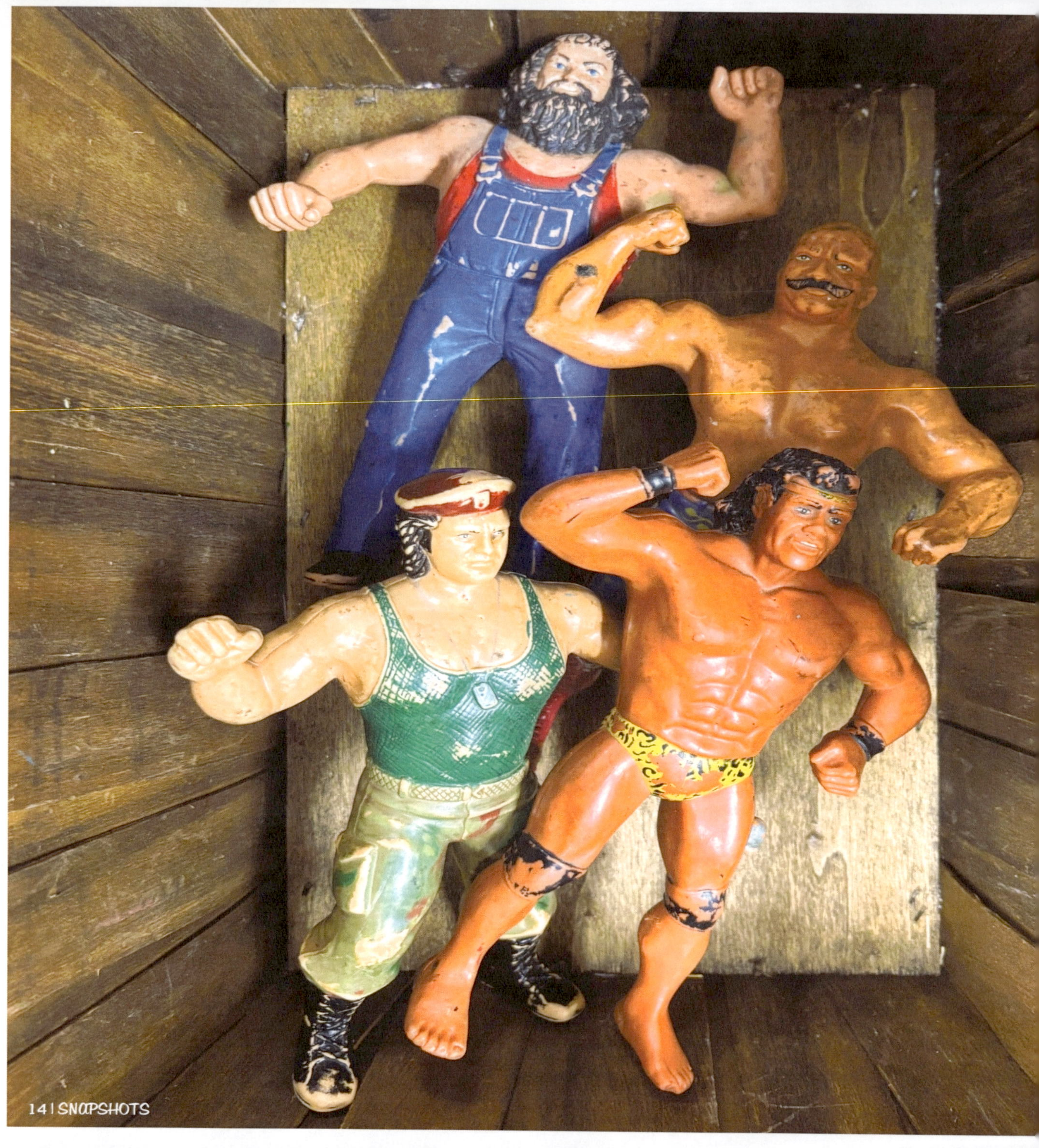

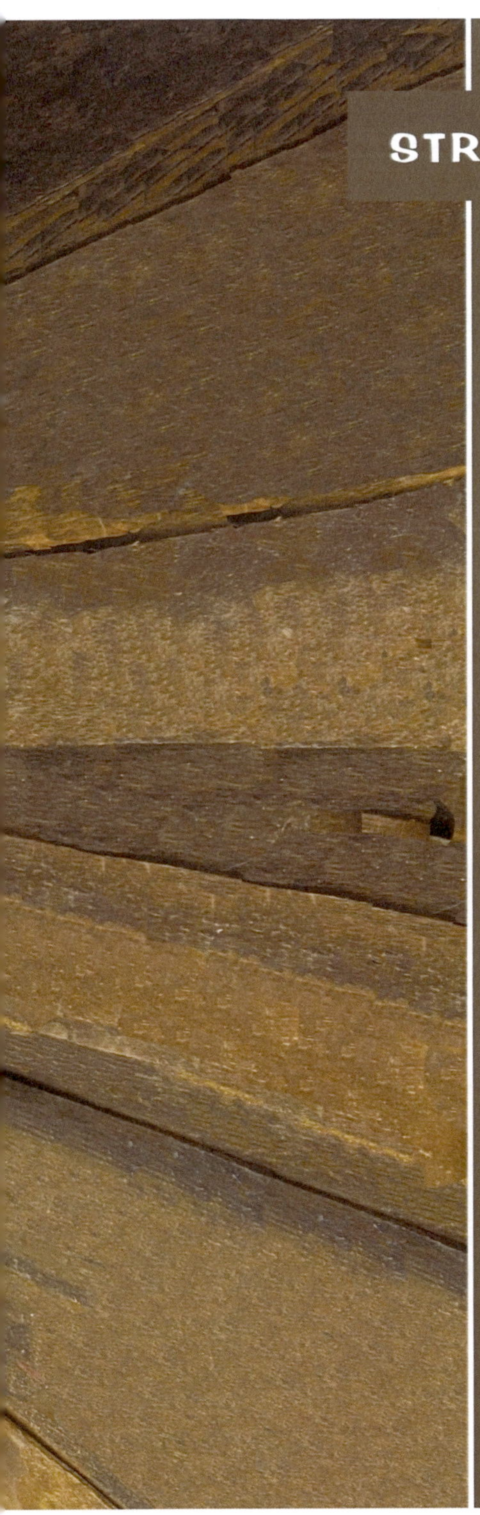

STRONG MEN

It takes a King to create and maintain
                  A healthy environment;
A Warrior to embody courage, strength and
                  Discipline;
A Magician to create positive change and
                  Transformation;
Love to embody passion, intimacy and
                  Connection;
And four Strong Men action figures
                  Laying in a wooden bin
At the consignment shop
                  To remind me to enact
The four masculine archetypes
                  Of my personality

OUR FACES ARE MASKS

Our faces are masks, says Buddha
A constructed persona, rather than
A true reflection of our inner self

My reinterpretation of childhood
Is contorted in the hustle of a stranger's smile
Of different ages
Yet we all live in the same age
Of Kali Yuga

Longings to kill are childhood nightmares
You know I should be alive
Pulling off my mask, I
Stare up at the Winter Zodiac
On Grand Central Terminal's famous ceiling
Admiring a true reflection
Of my inner self

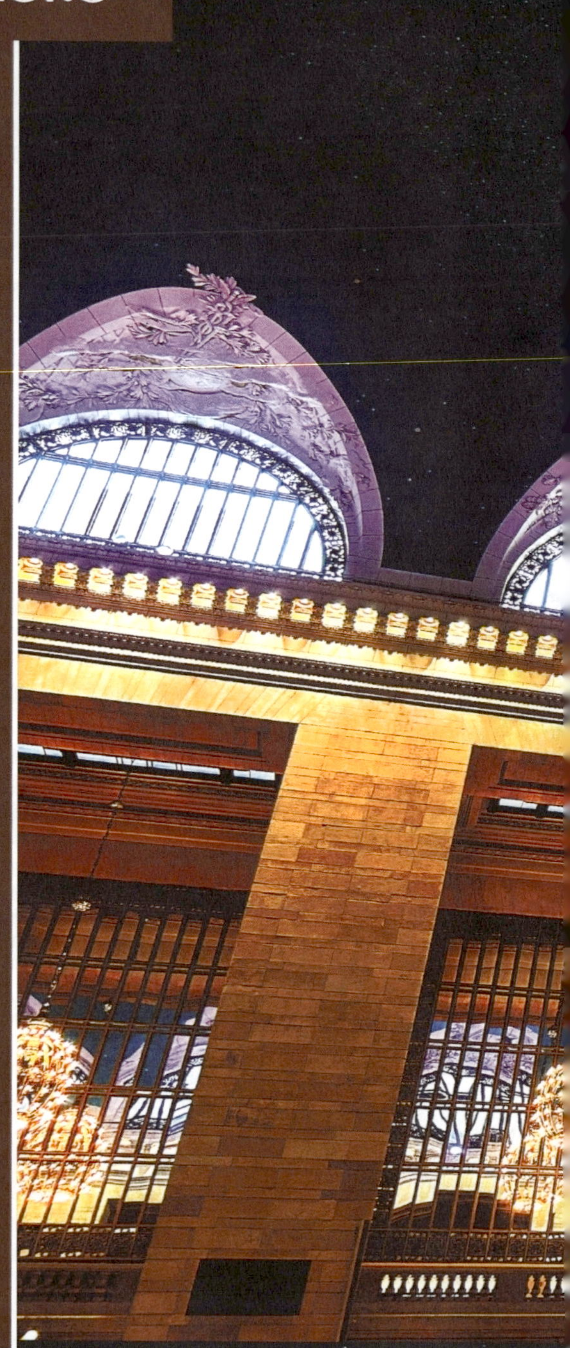

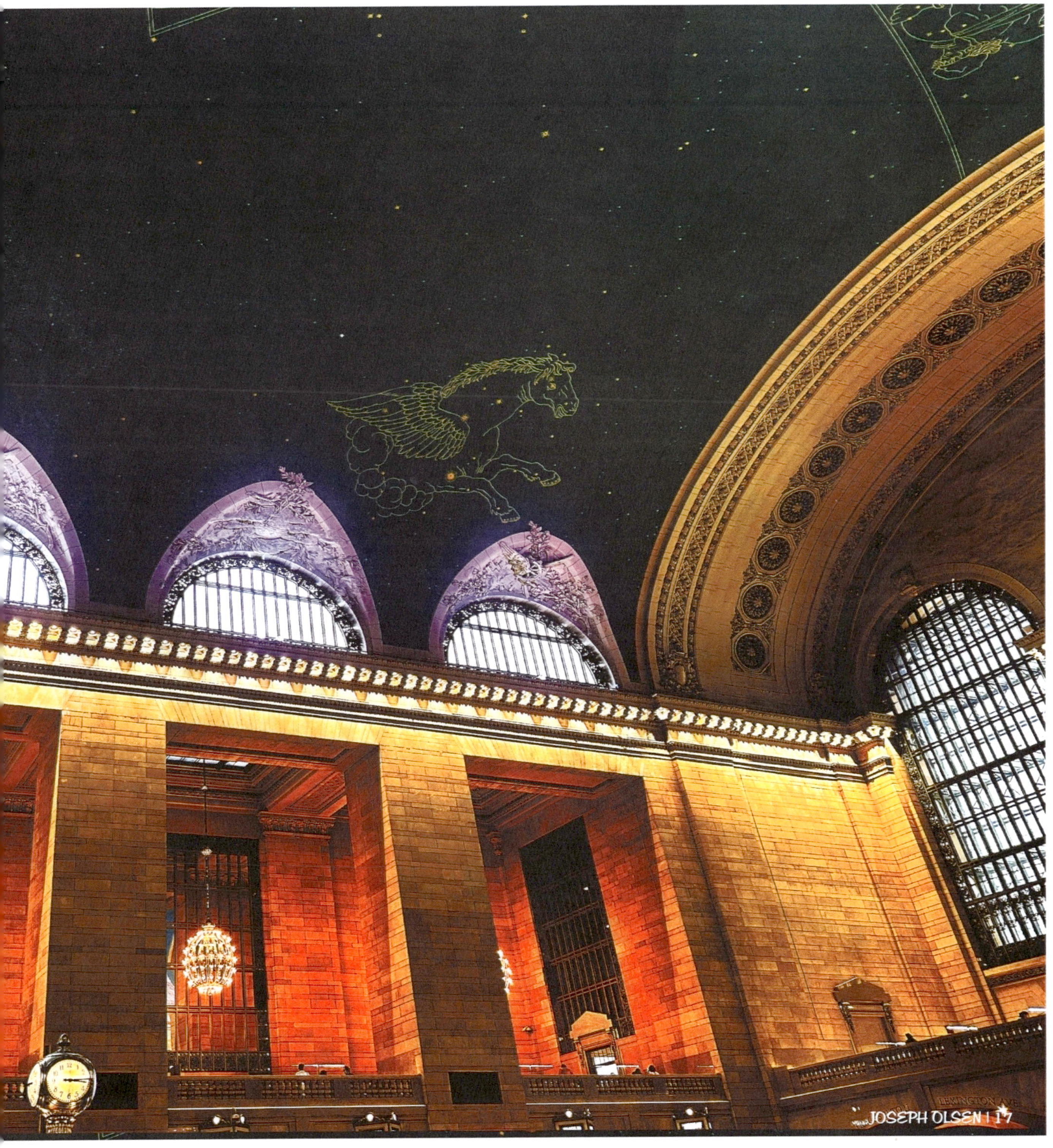
JOSEPH OLSEN | 17

HAIKU 8 - 14

8.
Out of the blue
A gang of clouds
Snuff out the sun

9.
Laughing like
A shooting
Star

10.
Laborers begin their weekend
Like children on summer break
Friday evening

11.
My daughter digs
Aimless excavating
Sandbox play

12.
At childhood's end
An adult
Changes a flat tire

13.
Early evening whistles
Boom!
The 5th of July

14.
Words are tiny black
Marks on a page
A night of stars, too

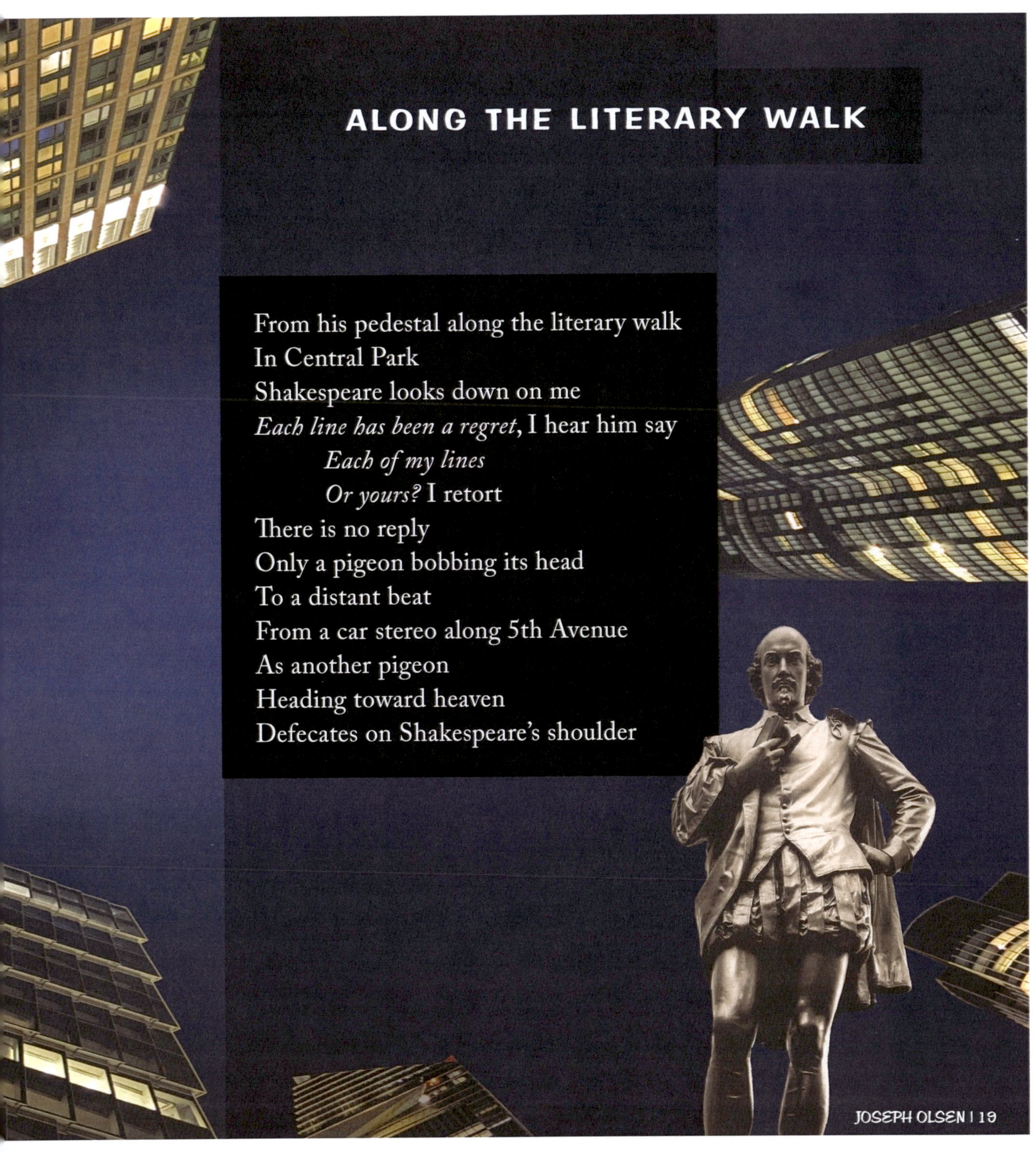

From his pedestal along the literary walk
In Central Park
Shakespeare looks down on me
Each line has been a regret, I hear him say
        Each of my lines
        Or yours? I retort
There is no reply
Only a pigeon bobbing its head
To a distant beat
From a car stereo along 5th Avenue
As another pigeon
Heading toward heaven
Defecates on Shakespeare's shoulder

VACATE THE PREMISES

To all the material things
Deemed practical by the world
He applied himself

Clean shaven and professionally dressed
He tapped a steady income
Drove daily to a nine-to-five
In the modern equivalent of
An ancient chariot
He made a house his home

But the sweat shop fabric
Of worldly financial and social gain
Quickly wore away at the seams
And he came undone

Unshaven and raggedly dressed
He tapped out a steady income
Broke down nine-to-five

Deserted like an ancient chariot
A notice from the bank
On a house he made his home
Ordered him to sling his hook

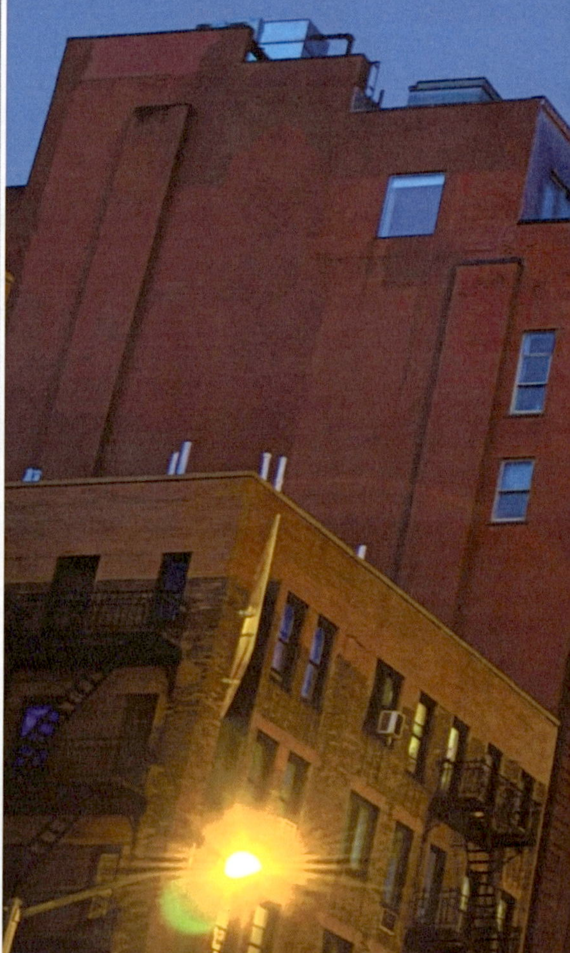

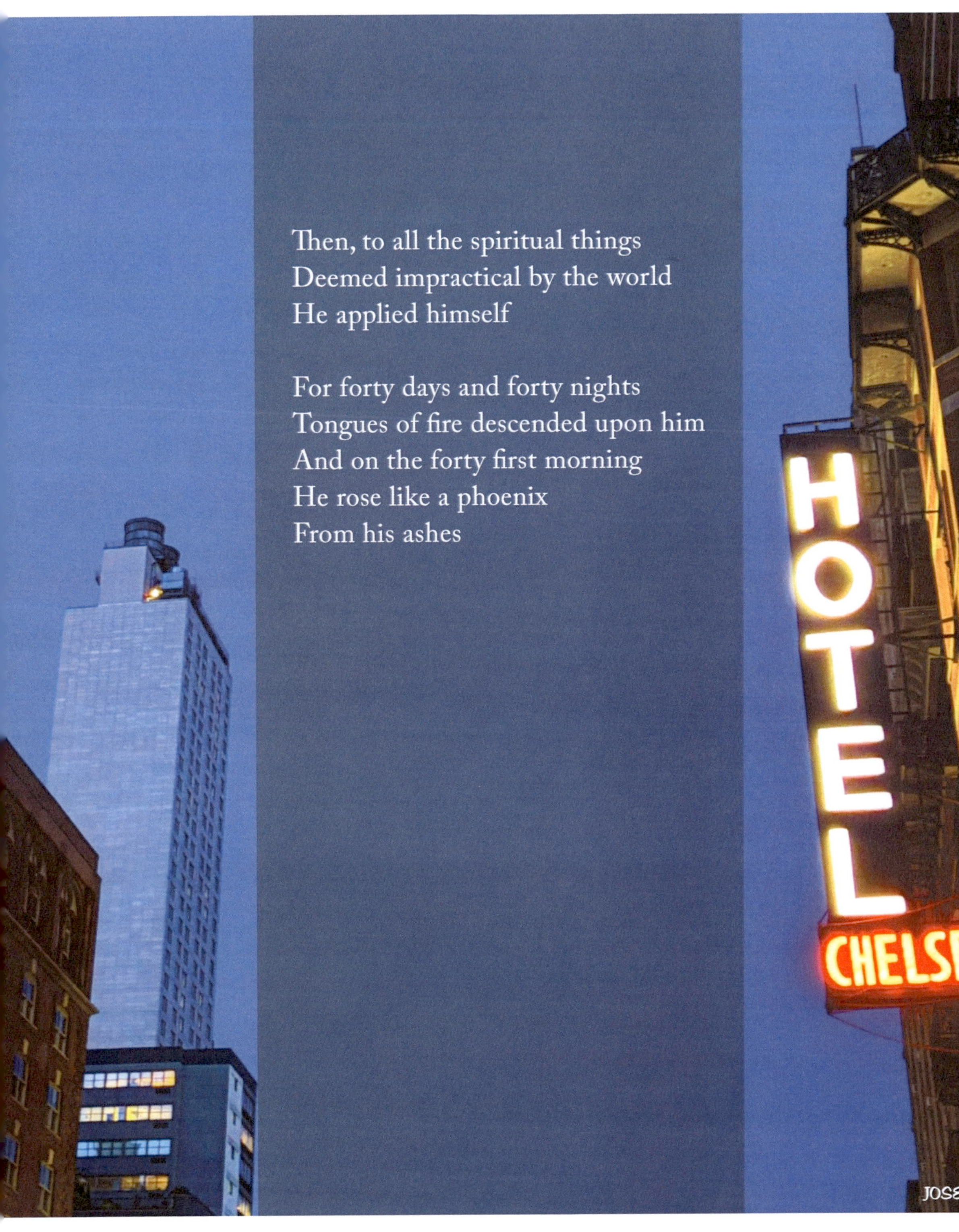

Then, to all the spiritual things
Deemed impractical by the world
He applied himself

For forty days and forty nights
Tongues of fire descended upon him
And on the forty first morning
He rose like a phoenix
From his ashes

MANSION TOUR

We enter through the chest cavity
Into the chambers of the heart
The roughly symmetrical, rounded shape
    Lends to the space
     A sense of serene elegance
Though, in this evening light
Scars from the great battles of love are prominent

Watch your step into the living room of the lungs
Extending across either side of the breast bone
Silent now, we breathe softly, slowly
Letting the self become still

Next, we come to the dining room of the stomach
The J-shaped area in the upper abdomen
Is grand and spacious, befitting
A gluttonous Standard American Diet
But be constantly mindful and know
When enough food has been taken
And all your afflictions will become slender

Climbing the grand staircase of the spine, at C1
We come to Golgotha, the skull

Into the Boudoir of the pupils
You'll notice, peering at the moon
The sympathetic nervous system
    Is triggered
Dilating the room
     Improving self-awareness
For when we see ourselves clearly
We are more confident and creative

Finally, we come between
The two hemispheres of the brain
    Into the pineal room
Opening the door to
    Higher consciousness
Our heart's truth begins to sing
    And our soul awakens

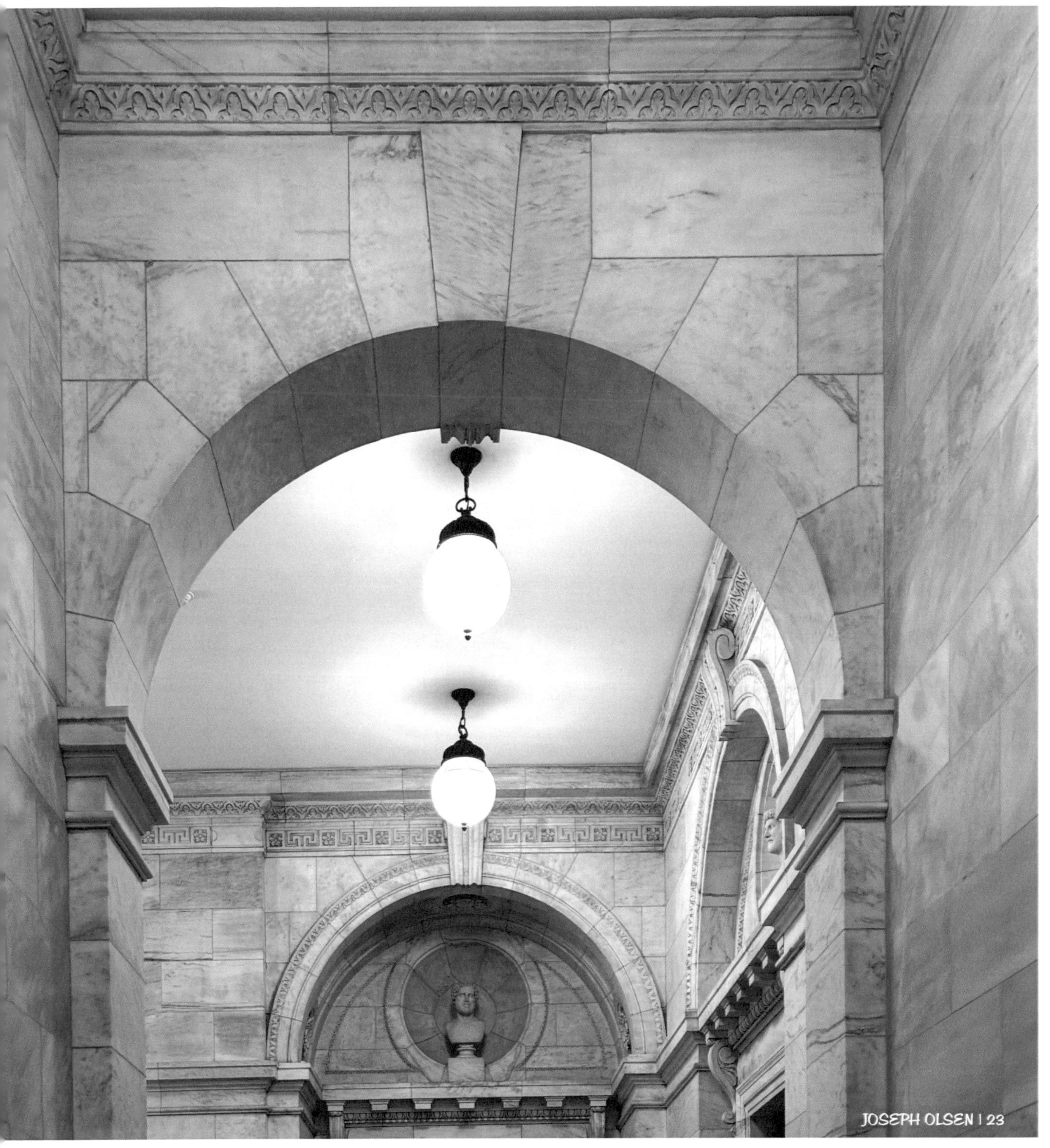

JOSEPH OLSEN | 23

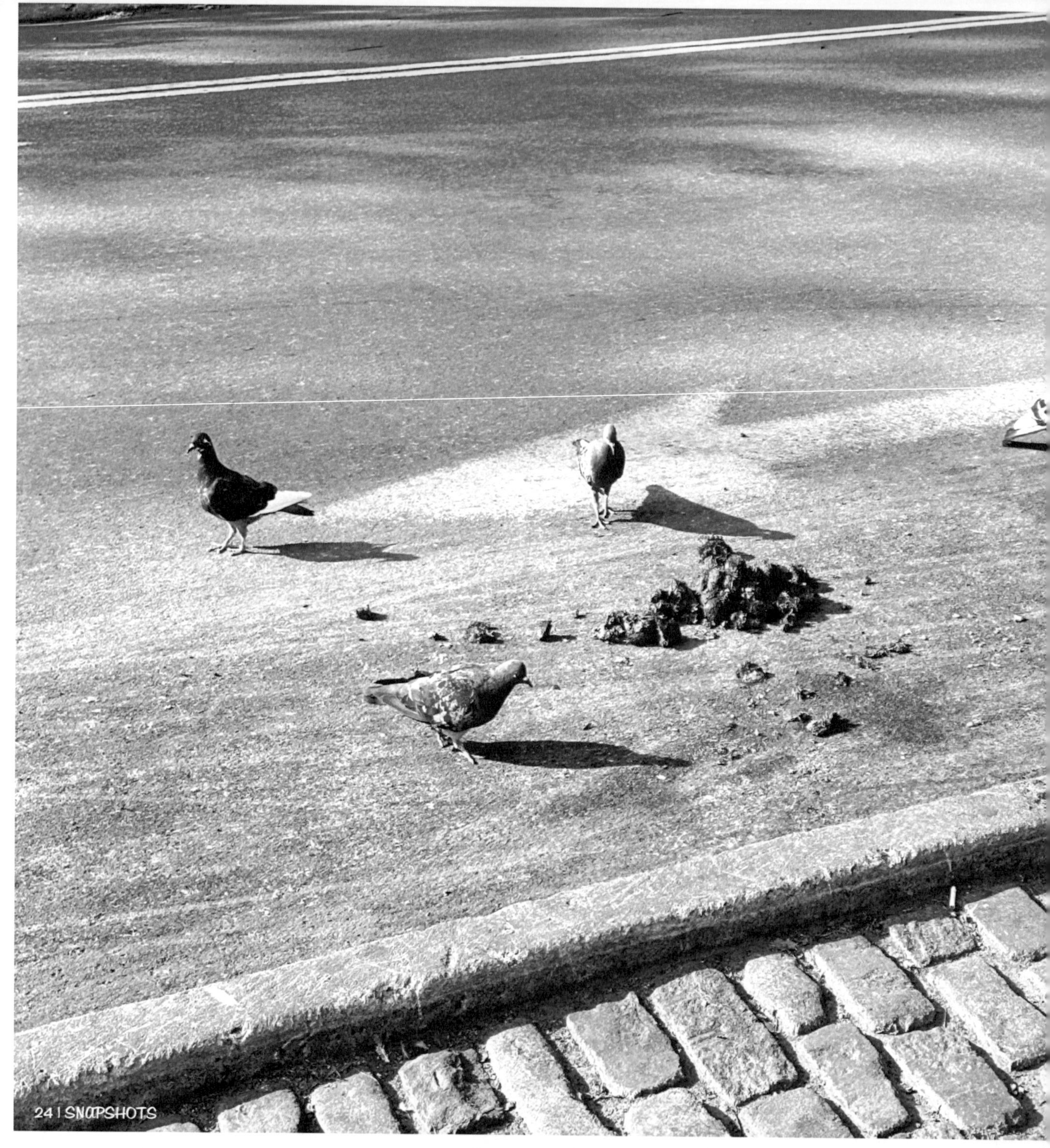

CENTRAL PARK MANURE

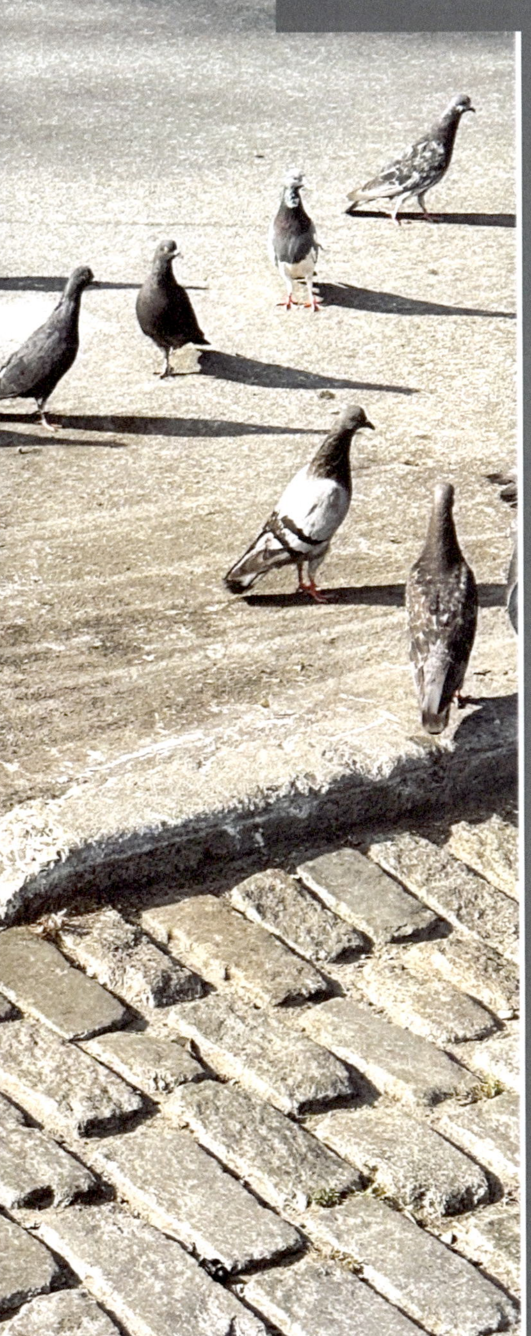

The horses drawing carriages in Central Park
Leave behind piles of manure
Despite requirements to use
Diapers or manure catchers to ease the
Complaints from park users and this cyclist
Who stopped to chew out a carriage driver
You're making the park hazardous, he says
Especially when it's mixed with puddles of rain
The carriage driver airs complaints of his own
I'm not stealing away profit for diapers
Nor catching the horse's shit, now move along
To which the cyclist sucks his teeth and
Peddles off

And as I snap a photo of pigeons pecking through
A fresh pile of manure for undigested crumbs
A tourist informs me, like a newspaper headline
That NYPD has increased patrols in Central Park
Following spikes in robberies

PUSHED TO FLY

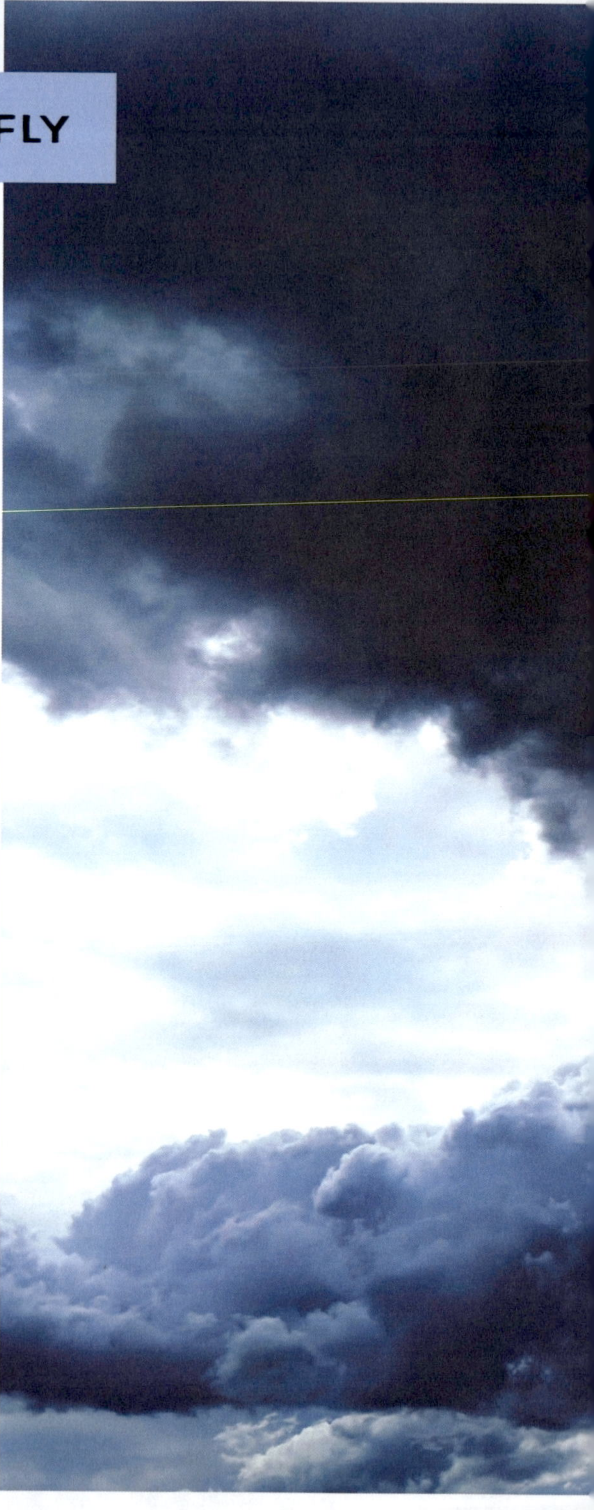

It's rough when you can't fly
Living a lie
On the ground, smelling morning roses
Searching for Jesus' entrance to Paradise
But it's evening and the roses are wilted and
Jesus' entrance to Paradise is beyond the sky
And it's rough when you can't fly
Living a lie
Like midnight roses under artificial light
You on your death bed
Acquiring the wings to take flight
But are too terrified to leave the ground
Enamored in a lie
Having to be pushed to fly

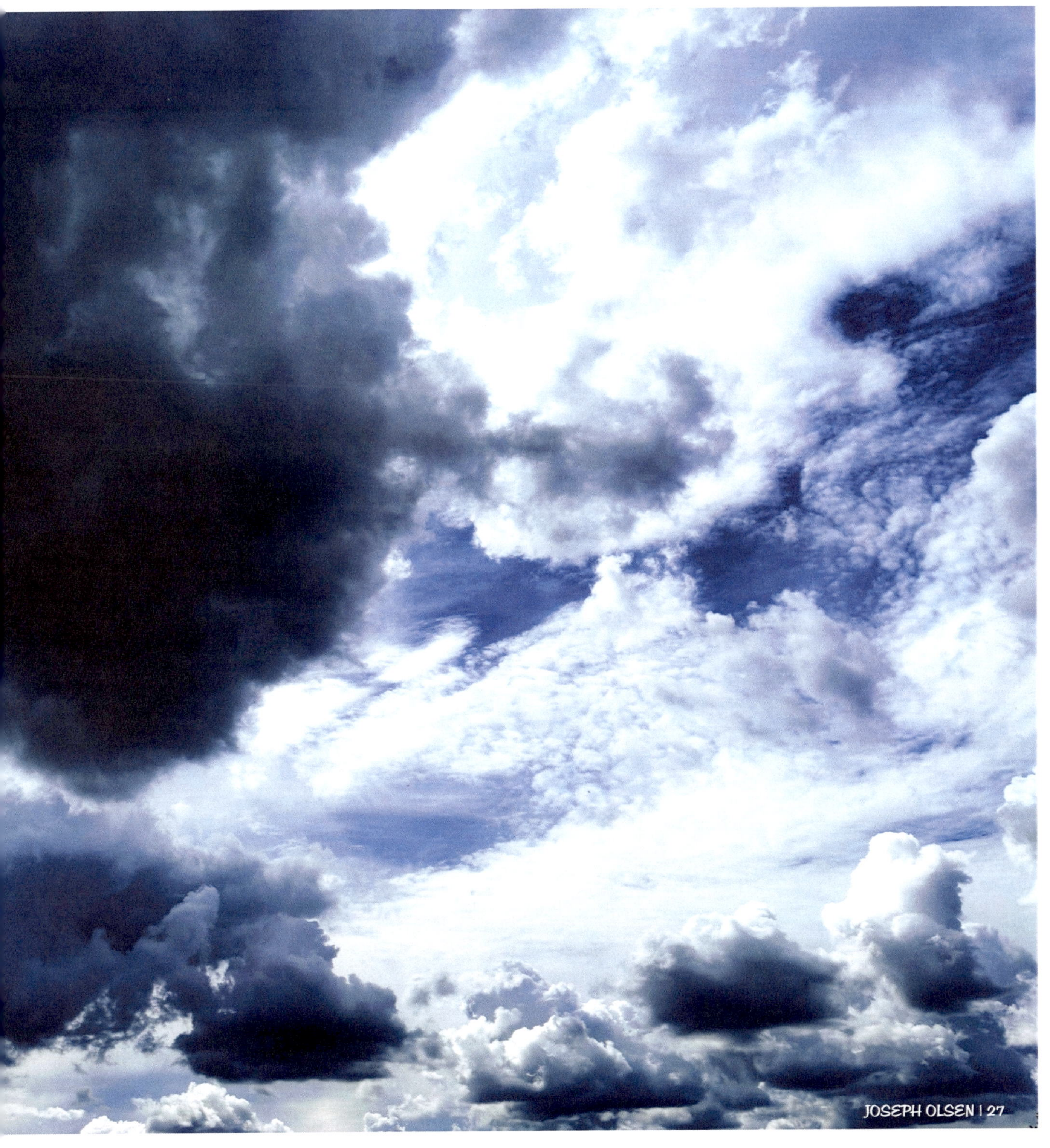
JOSEPH OLSEN | 27

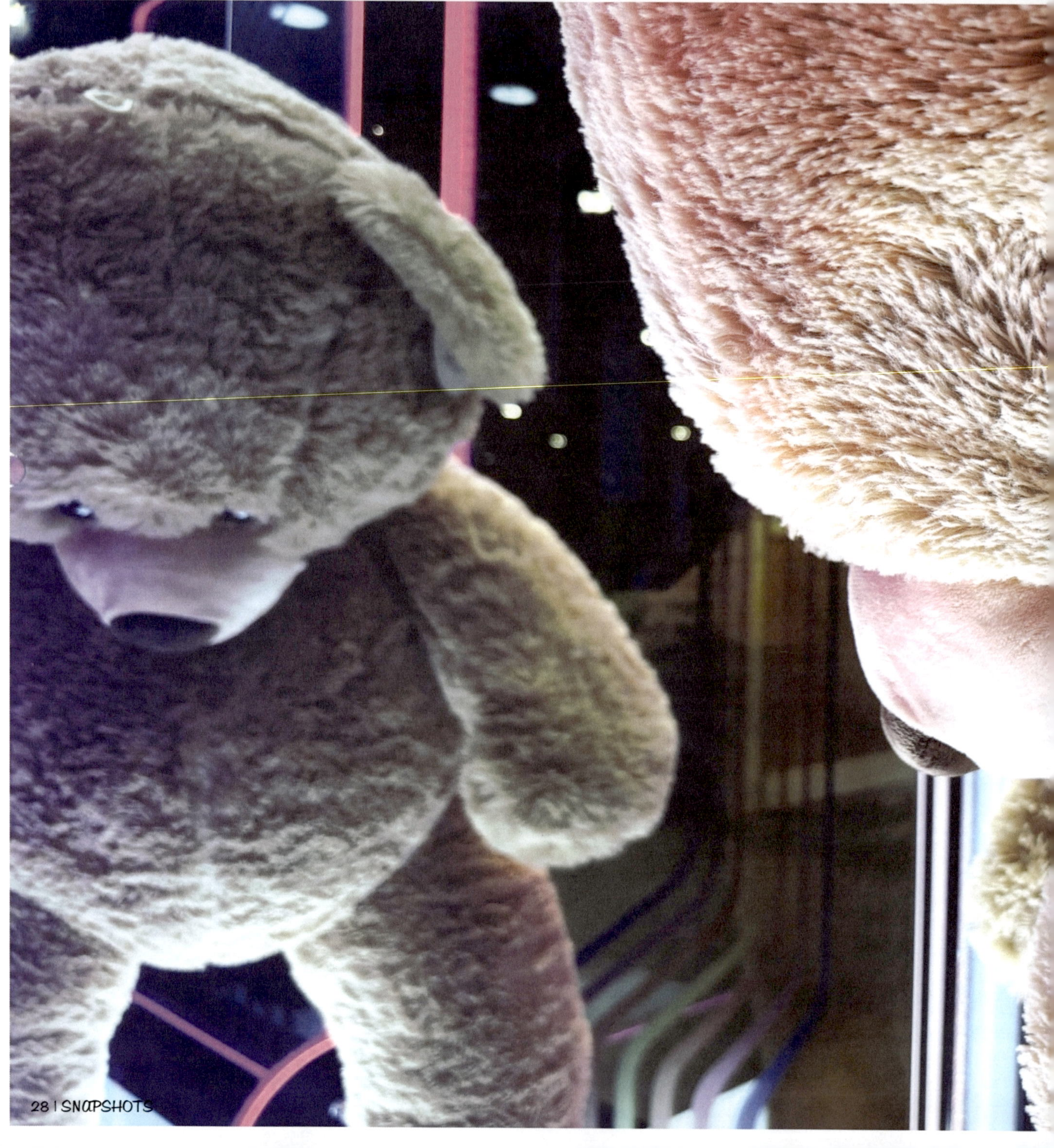

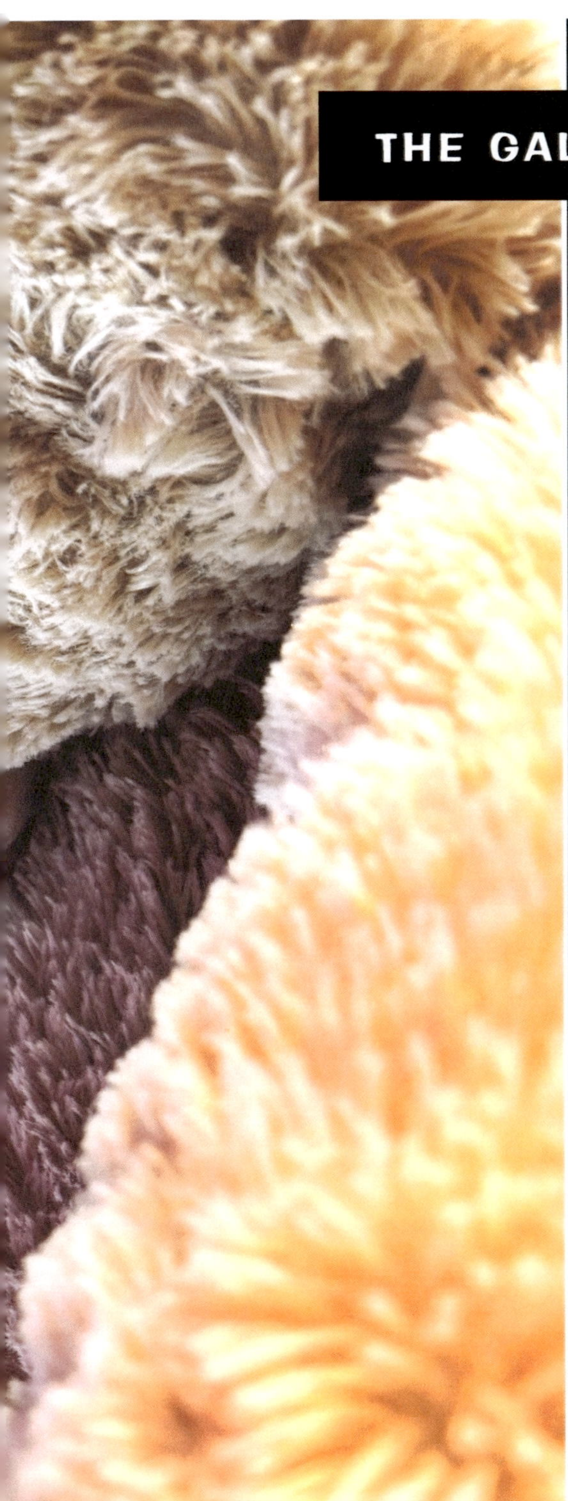

Hanging from the gallows
                Of the arcade
A child's most wanted criminal
                Is out of breath
If I am *lucky* to win him, I'll
                Stuff him in a grave
And pray for quick conveyance
                Of his soul

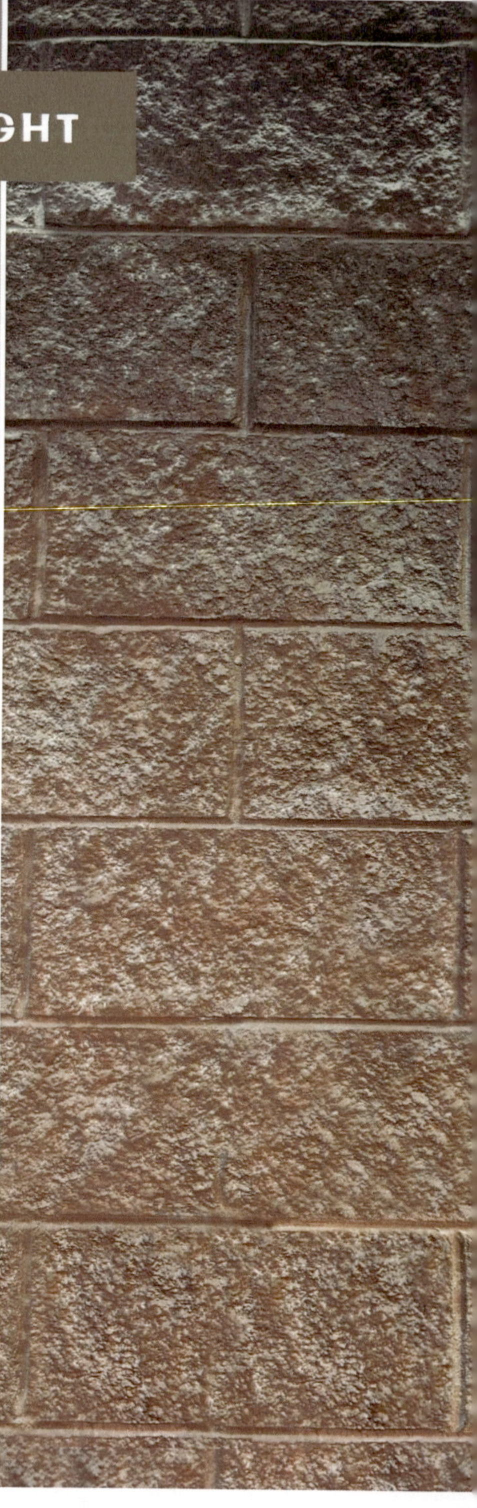

YOUR OWN LIGHT

Dancing for the wallflowers
    On the verge of blooming tonight
    In the moonlight
    That pours forth like your own light

Dancing for the meaning
    Of loss
    In a funeral procession
    Mourning your own physical corpse

Dancing for the angels
    Minutes before final judgment
    In tight formation
    Battling against your own enslavement

Dancing for the bull
    Seeing red in a cockfight
    In the sunlight
    That pours forth like your own light

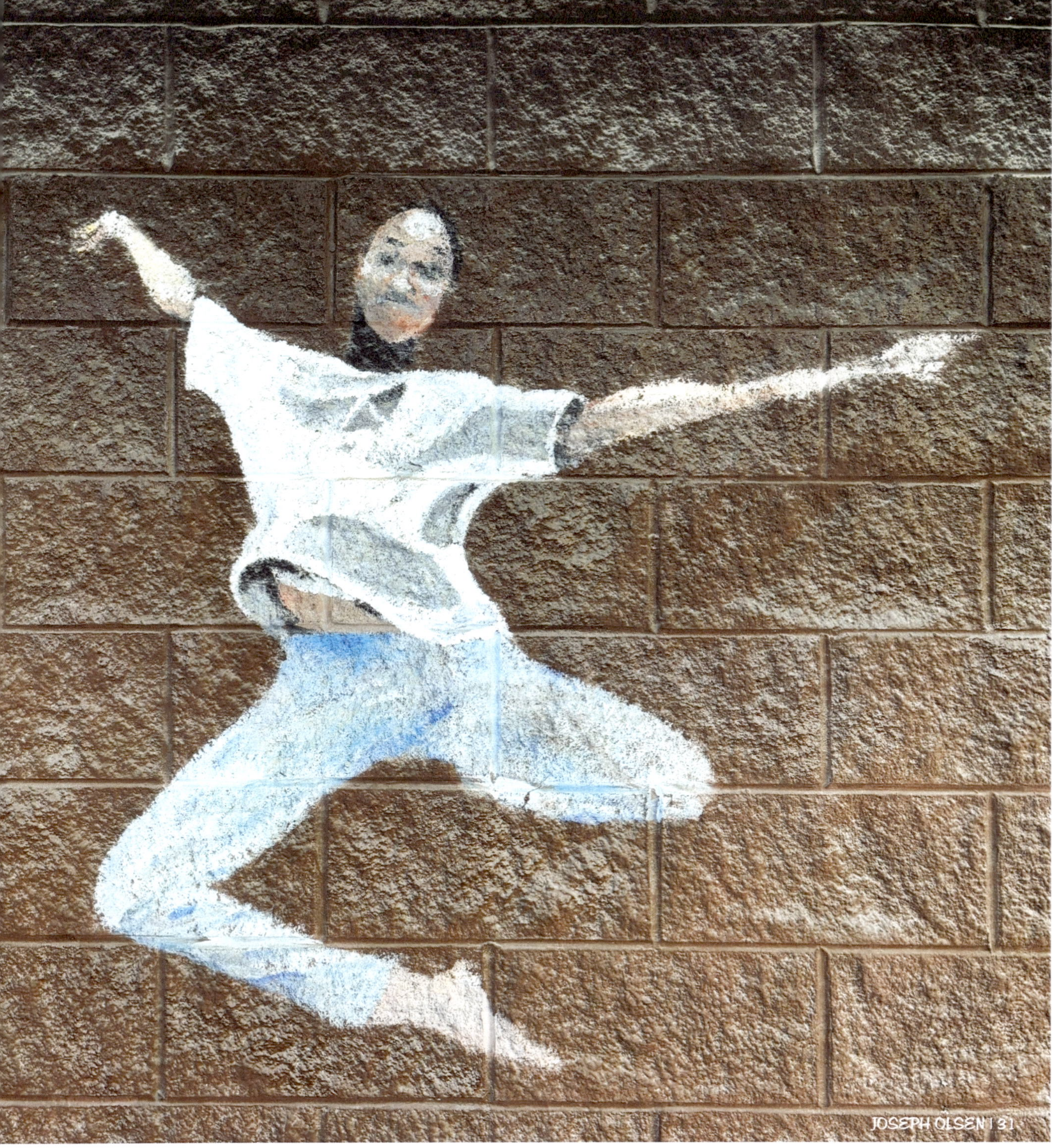

JOSEPH OLSEN 31

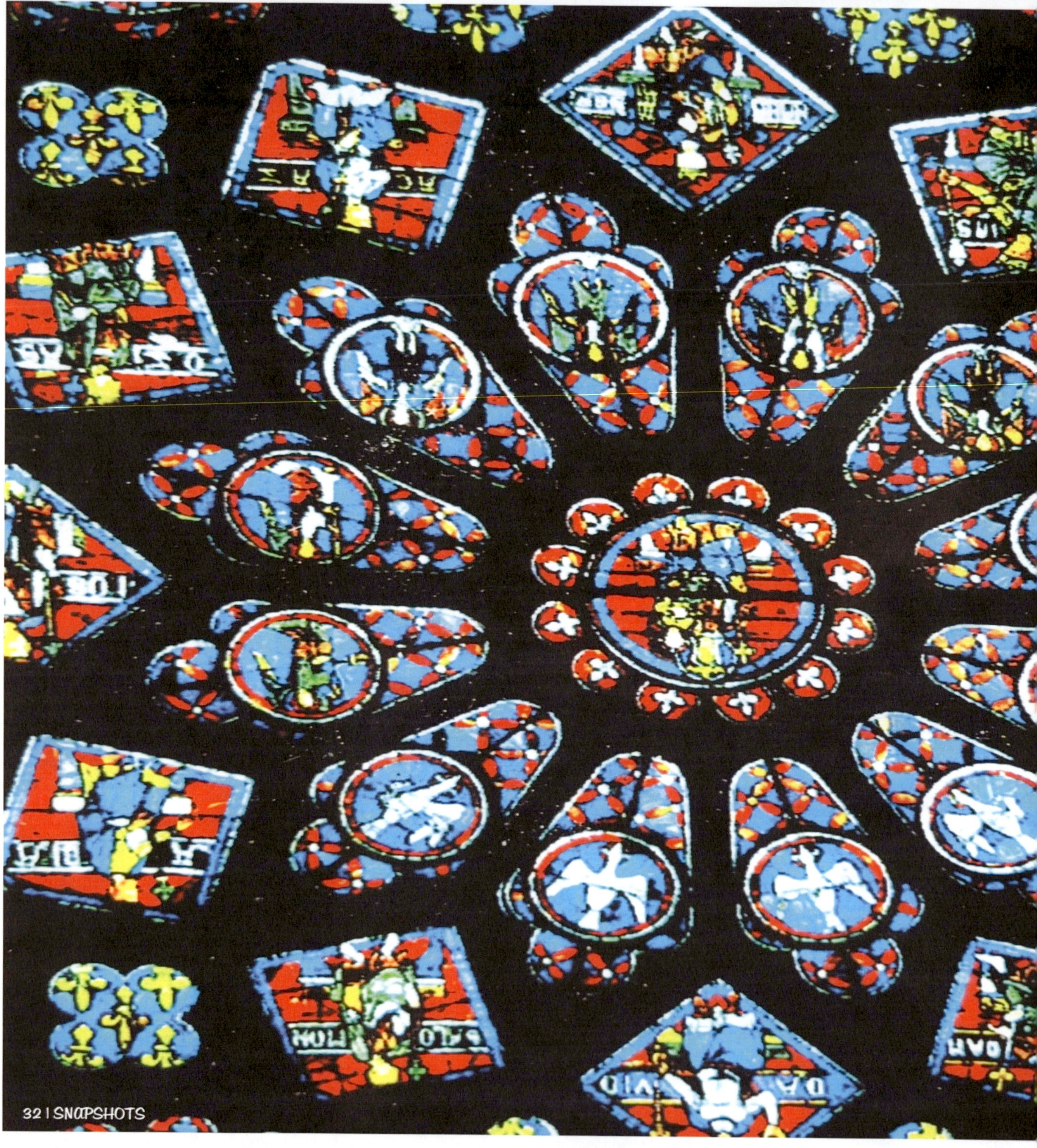

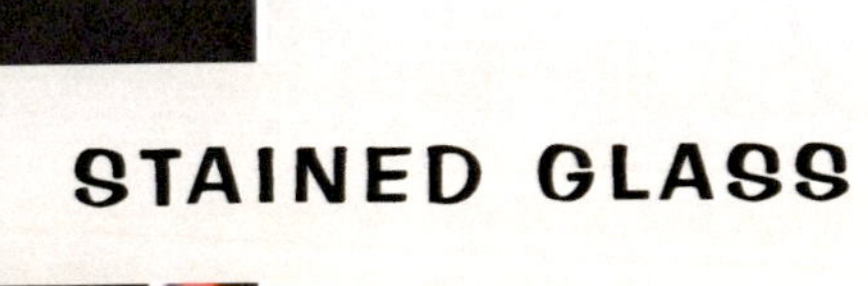

STAINED GLASS

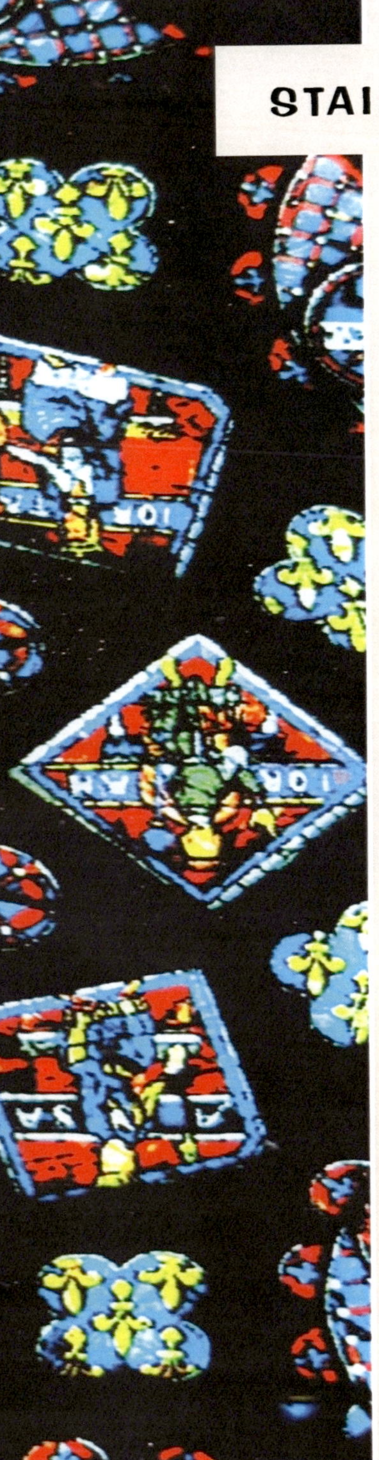

As the symbol of a dove
The grace of the holy spirit enters
Inside you, like vapors into clouds
The permutation of the soul
Is taking shape
Unlimited and easy
Too sweet for war
Blessed with a present heart
Beating in morning sunlight
Emanating love eternal
Stained glass of the most high

GAME OF LIFE

Beginning the rat race
In a first edition poker glare
Contorting a Pictionary of smiles, frowns
Heartache, loss and grief
Predictable moves in distress
The classic sorry remains
An apology too late to express
Spinning for wealth in ill health
Rolling the dice for a wage, passing go
Monopolizing stranger things
Chess pawns in forward flow
Striving to stack the odds in our favor
Until the mind topples in an evening of Jenga
Ending the rat race
In a final edition poker stare
Face up under a field of crimson clover

GAME OVER

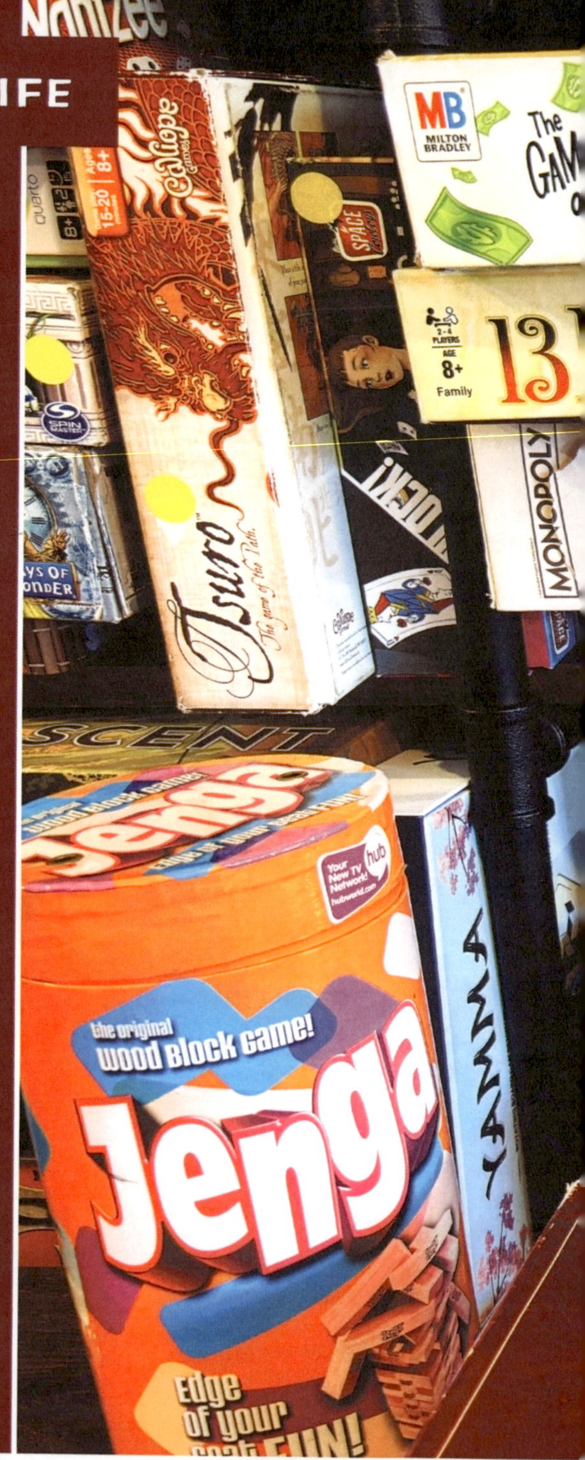

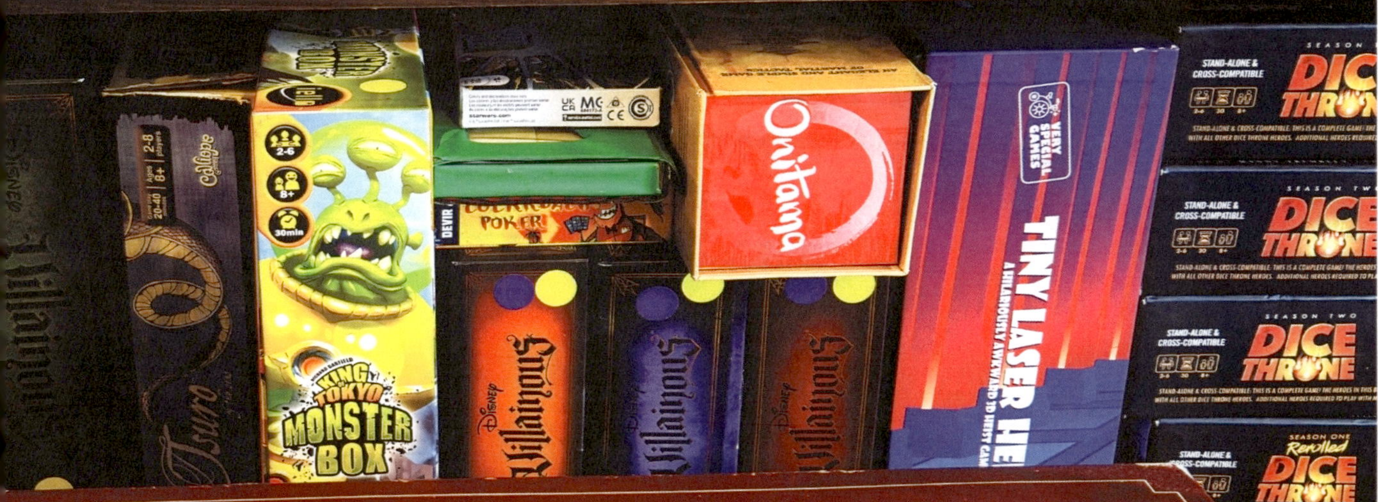
Frozen
Surprise Slides
Game
A Very Thinky Game for 2 Clever Cats
boop.
smirk
Family
AGES 9+
F E
Classic SORRY!
6+
EnD DRIVE
Blokus TRIGON
For 2 to 4 Players
Ages 5 to Adult
Educational Insights
Blokus TRIGON
STRANGER THINGS
COLLECTOR'S EDITION
MONOPOLY
The Classic Edition
2-8 players
Ages 8+
20-40
Calliope
2-6
8+
30min
KING of TOKYO
MONSTER BOX
Tsuro
COCKROACH POKER
DEVIR
Disney Villainous
Disney Villainous
Disney Villainous
Onitama
STAND-ALONE & CROSS-COMPATIBLE
VERY SPECIAL GAMES
TINY LASER HE
A HILARIOUSLY AWKWARD 3D HEIST GAM
SEASON
DICE THRONE
STAND-ALONE & CROSS-COMPATIBLE
SEASON TWO
DICE THRONE
STAND-ALONE & CROSS-COMPATIBLE
SEASON TWO
DICE THRONE
STAND-ALONE & CROSS-COMPATIBLE
SEASON ONE
ReRolled
DICE THRONE
PICTIONARY
THE GAME OF QUICK DRAW
SECOND EDITION

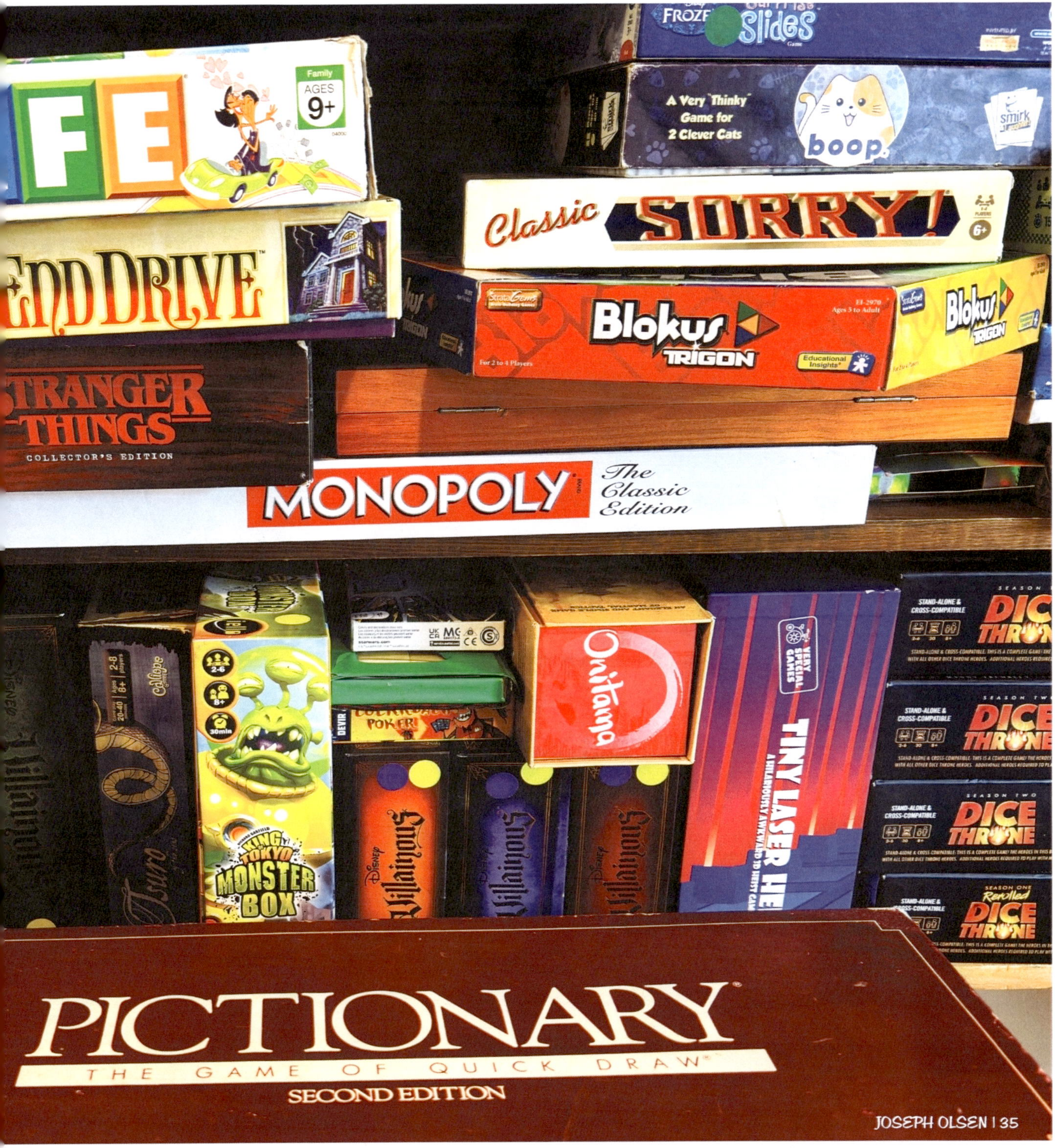

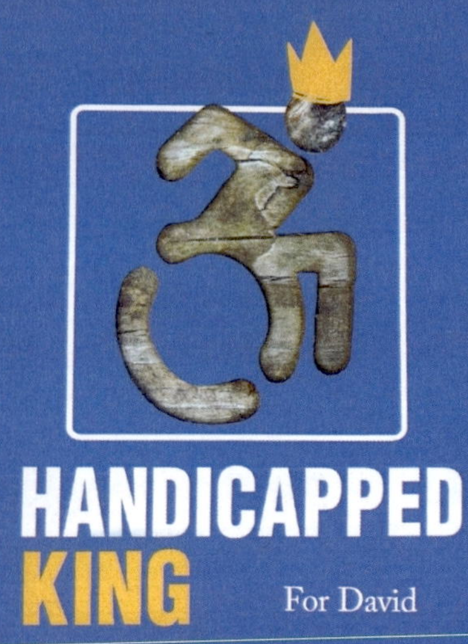

HANDICAPPED KING

For David

I stop by to drop off the documentary
Forks Over Knives
When my *brother*
Bending my ear with five and dime grievances
Tells me he can't get right with Jehovah
That he's being punished
For all the wrong he did in life
Then, with the weight of an overdue load
His weak, stick figure legs buckle
                        To the bathroom
Back to the Living room
He collapses onto his throne
In front of the television
Nursing his wounds with the jesters
Of Comedy Central
Tumbling down the rabbit hole
Of streams on YouTube
Maintaining his meager empire
With Walmart's *great value* meats and dairy
Chasing down pills prescribed
For lack of sleep, the burning
Sensations, brittle bones
Anxiety, constipation, headaches
                        This whole time
A New World Translation of the Holy Scriptures

Is sitting on the side table
You believe the Bible is divinely revealed truth?
He chuckles, coughs, *It's the word of God*
You shouldn't believe you're being punished then, I say
As the Bible emphasizes God's power to heal
And protect believers from illness
I point to the documentary
The immune system is a divinely appointed defense
Against pathogens and other threats to health
He picks it up, ridicules its
Proclamation to prevent or reverse chronic diseases
By adopting a whole-food
                              Plant-based diet
Then, setting it atop the Bible
He orders me out of his kingdom

Exiting, I consider
                              Mistranslated scripture
Hardening a King's heart, keeping him blind to
                              The writing on the wall

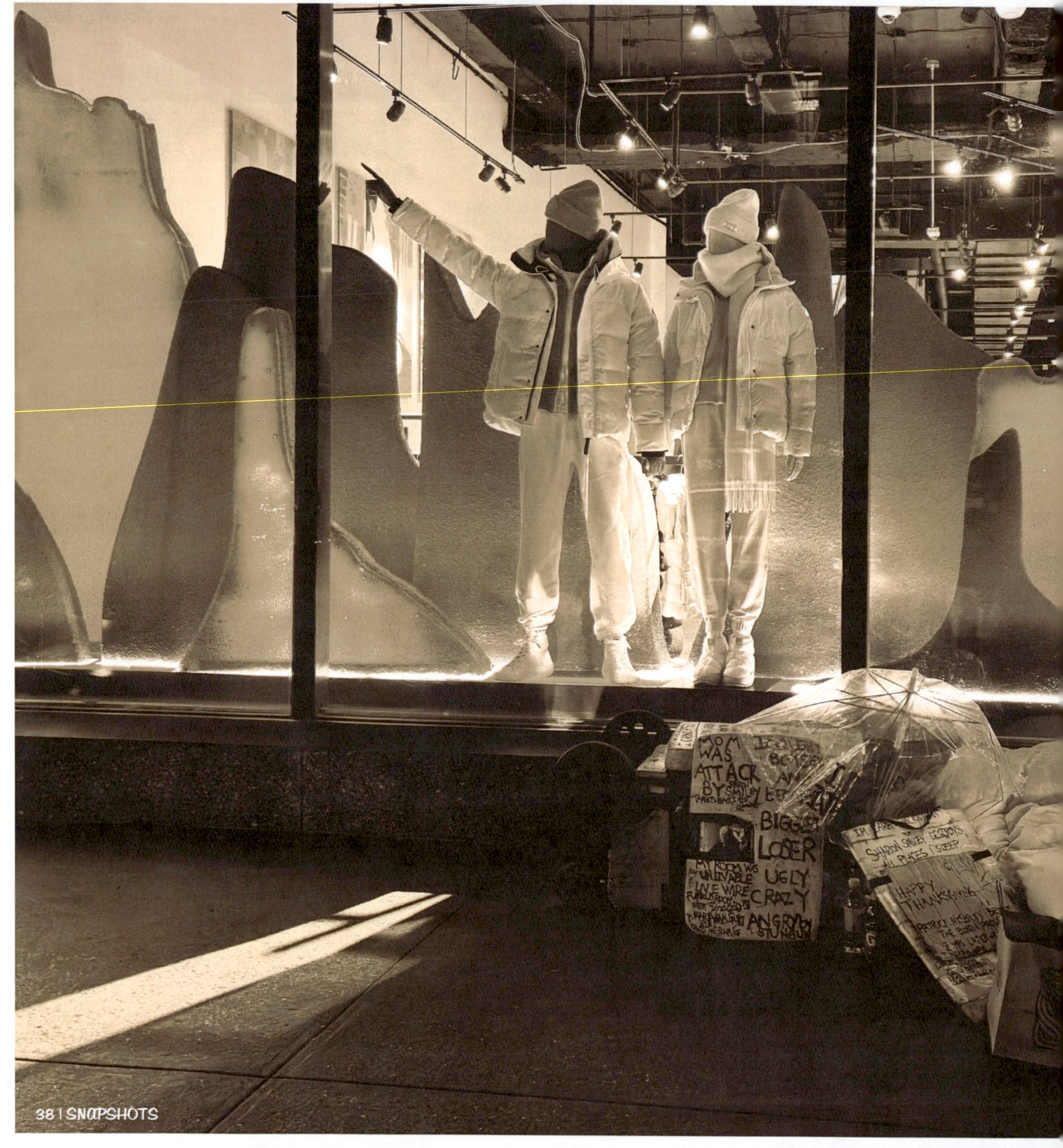

MOM WAS ATTACK BY SMILEY
BIGGE LOSER
MY ROOM WAS UNLIVABLE
LIVE WIRE
UGLY CRAZY
ANGRY STUNGUN
IM
SHARON SMILEY DESTROYS ALL PLACES I SLEEP
HAPPY THANKSGIVING

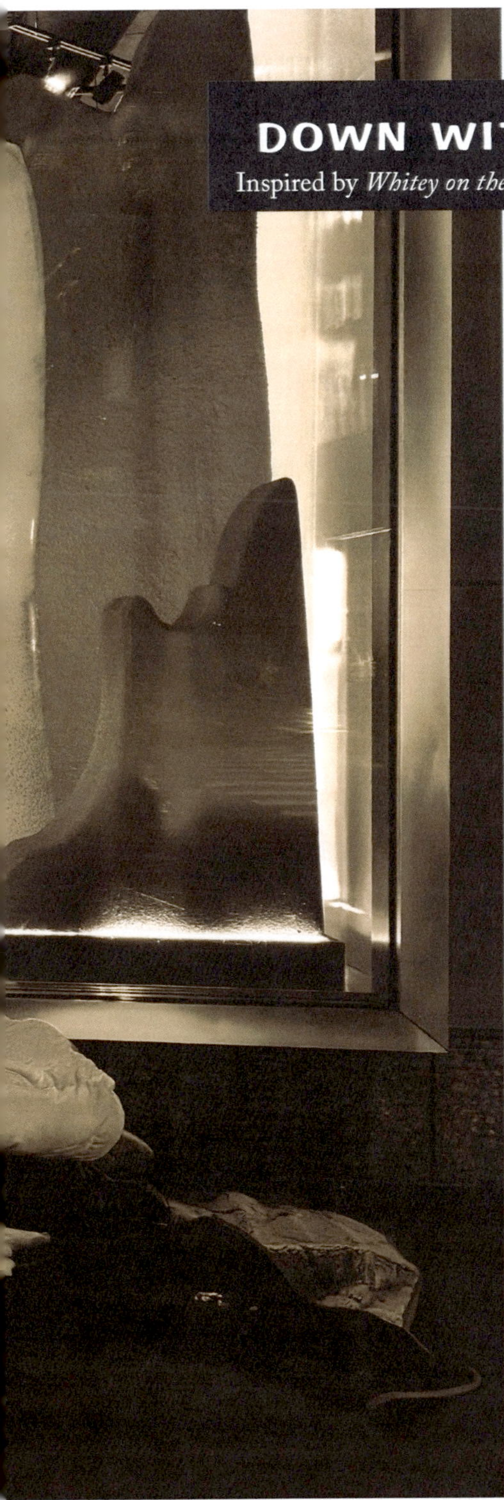

DOWN WITH WHITEY

Inspired by *Whitey on the Moon* by Gil Scott-Heron

Down with whitey
On the moon in sixty nine
Landing in a dream of molten silver
One giant leap from the kingdom of the divine

Down with politicians
Pitting the people against each other
Every unkept promise and idle word
Judge them, brother

Down with fallen angels
Clipped at high noon
The children commence sacrificing
On altars of cardboard strewn

Down with Heaven
The stars are brawling
Every beggar, destitute and chosen
Heed your true calling

Down with whitey
On the moon in sixty nine
Landing in a dream of molten silver
One giant leap from the kingdom of the divine

WHILE MOTHER AND BABY DAUGHTER SLEEP

For Amy & Aylin

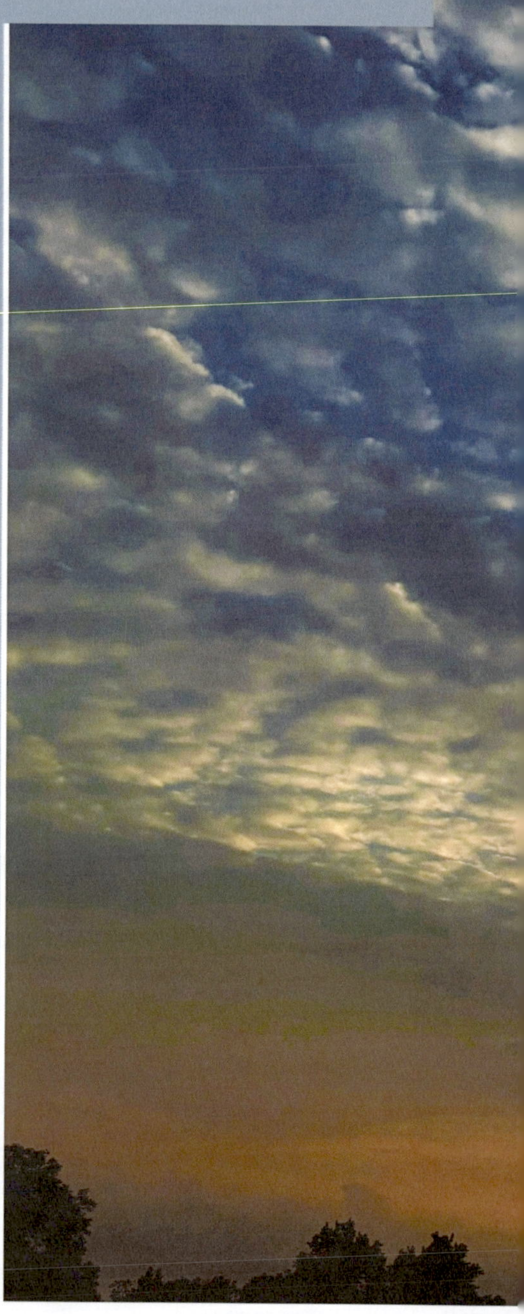

While mother and baby daughter sleep
In the sanctuary of sunset
Approaching moonrise
I take to the page

Mother dreaming the Old Testament
Finding solace in a jealous god
Baby daughter drawing innocent breath
In tender rebirth
Breathing that paradox of good and evil
Infinite, yet impermanent

As mother tosses and baby daughter turns
I remember words are as a honeycomb
Sweet to the soul

Mother begins whispering the secrets
Of the wind
Baby daughter begins composing the music
Of the clouds

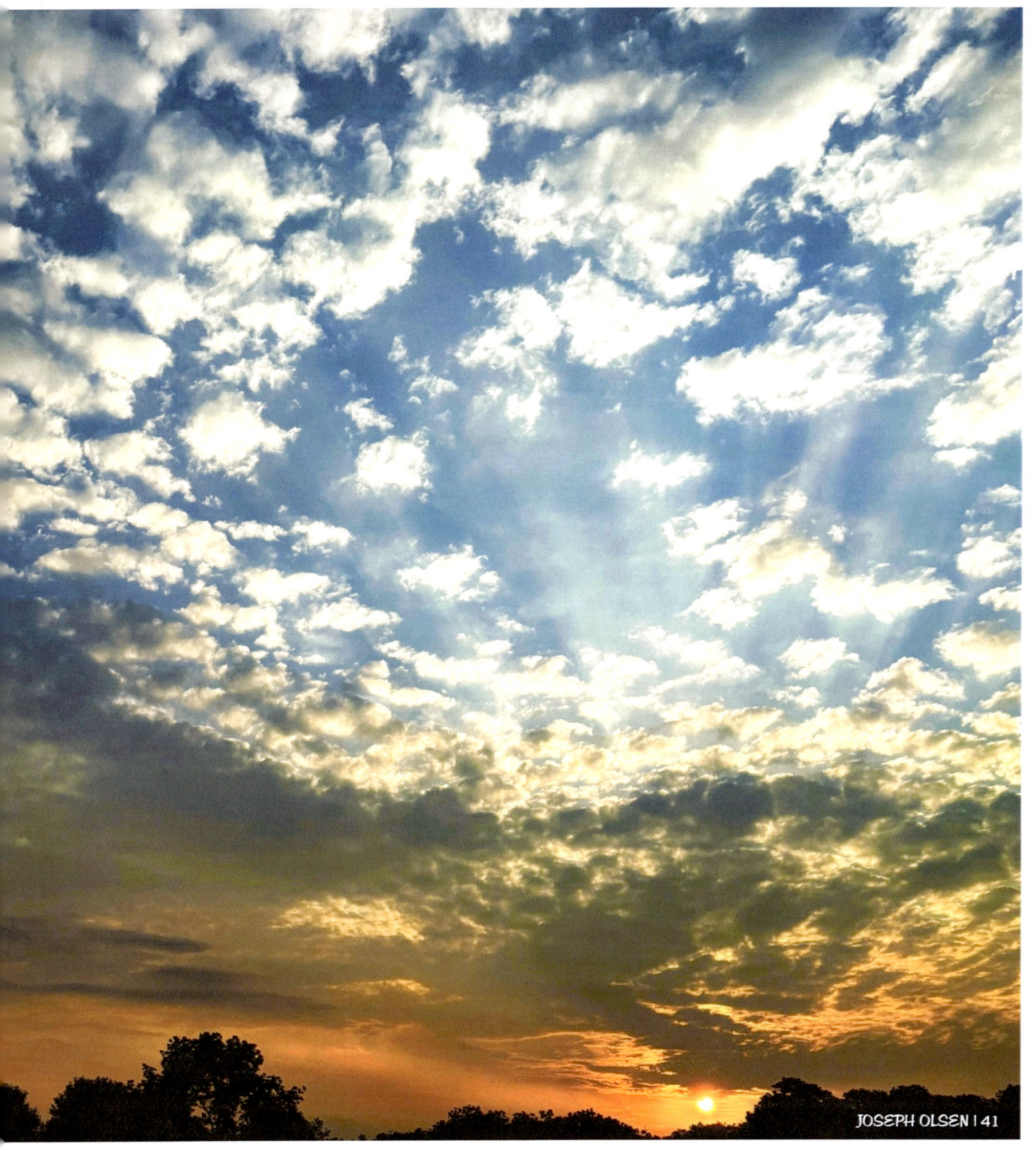
JOSEPH OLSEN | 41

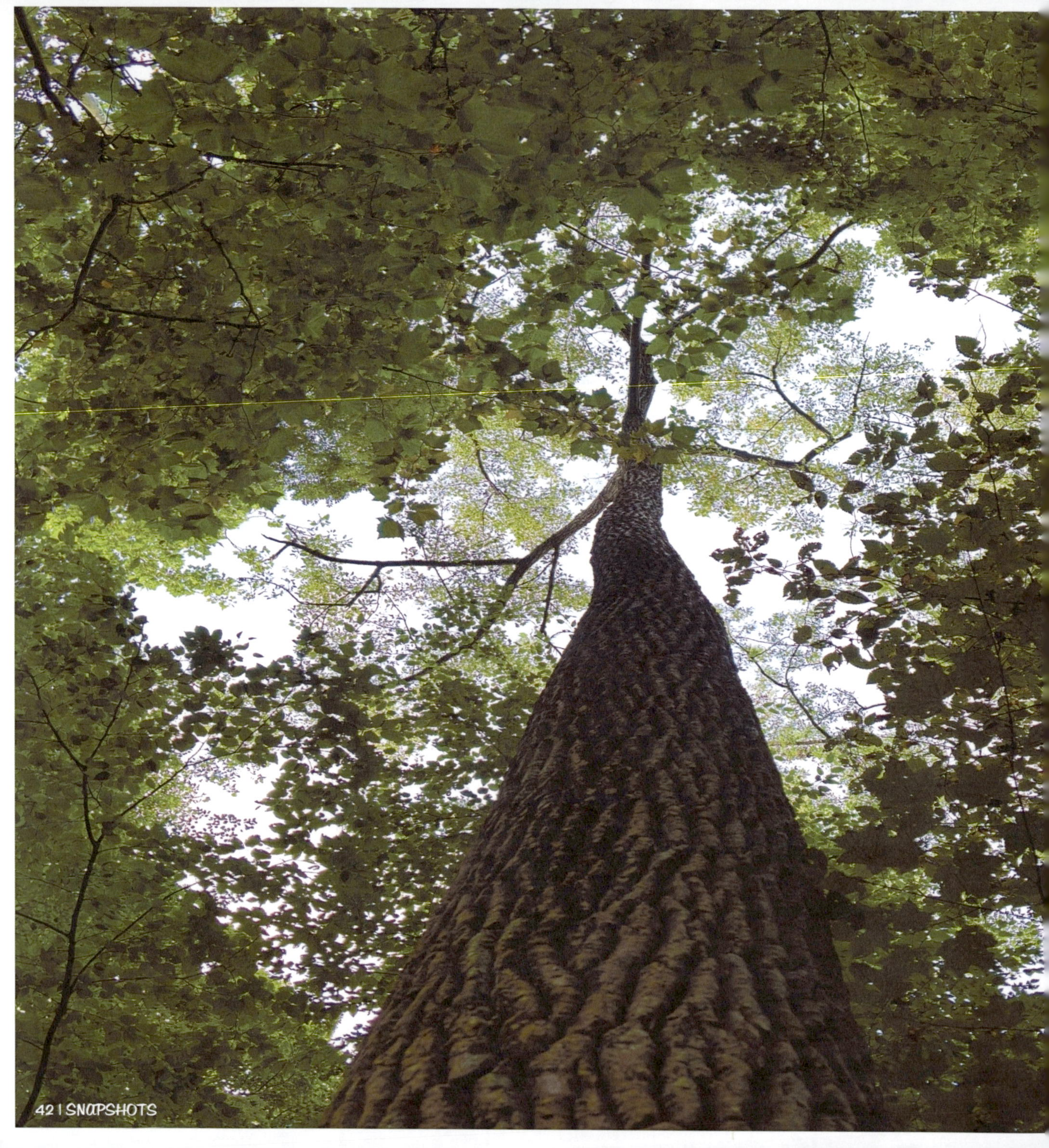

TILTING THE CAMERA UP

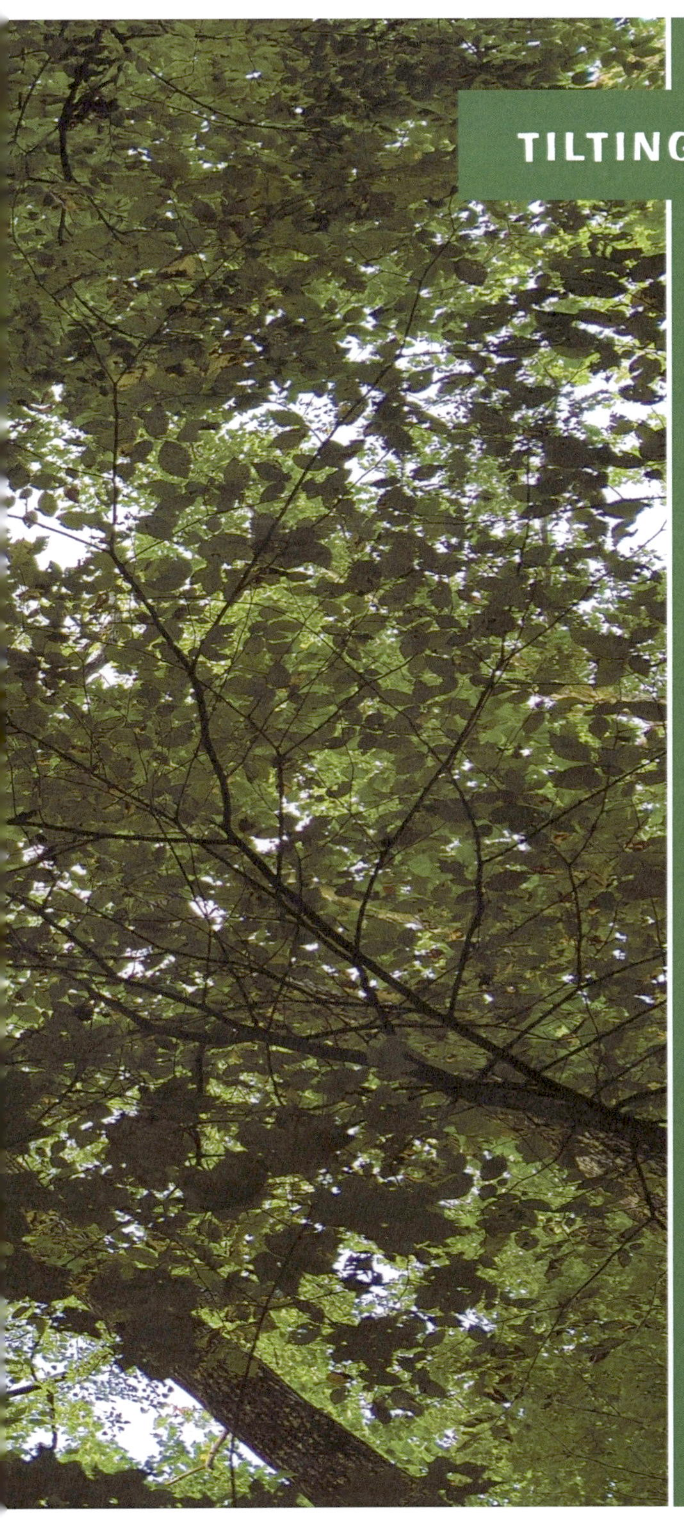

I was on the ground
Tilting the camera

Up
Picturing souls hunger

For the sevenfold
Peace of flesh

In the branches
Of the tall oak

Reaching for the
Sun

We were discussing
God, which

Is how we became
Human

HAIKU 15 - 19

15.
The experience of
Violence in the night
Otherwise, never known

16.
Of words and images
The enjoyment
Of an empty hour

17.
Each man pursues his own gain
And sells his own soul into slavery
How can there be peace?

18.
Compromised after an unsuccessful attack
One must now act very differently
A game of chess

19.
A decaffeinated conversation
Sipping watered down
Refill diner coffee

ONE MUST NOW ACT VERY DIFFERENTLY

HOW CAN THERE BE PEACE?

FIRST SIGHT

My first sight
Of evil at six
I saw myself as no-thing

It's simple enough:
A poem without
A page;

A tombstone
Without a grave;
A lover

Without
Memories
Of you

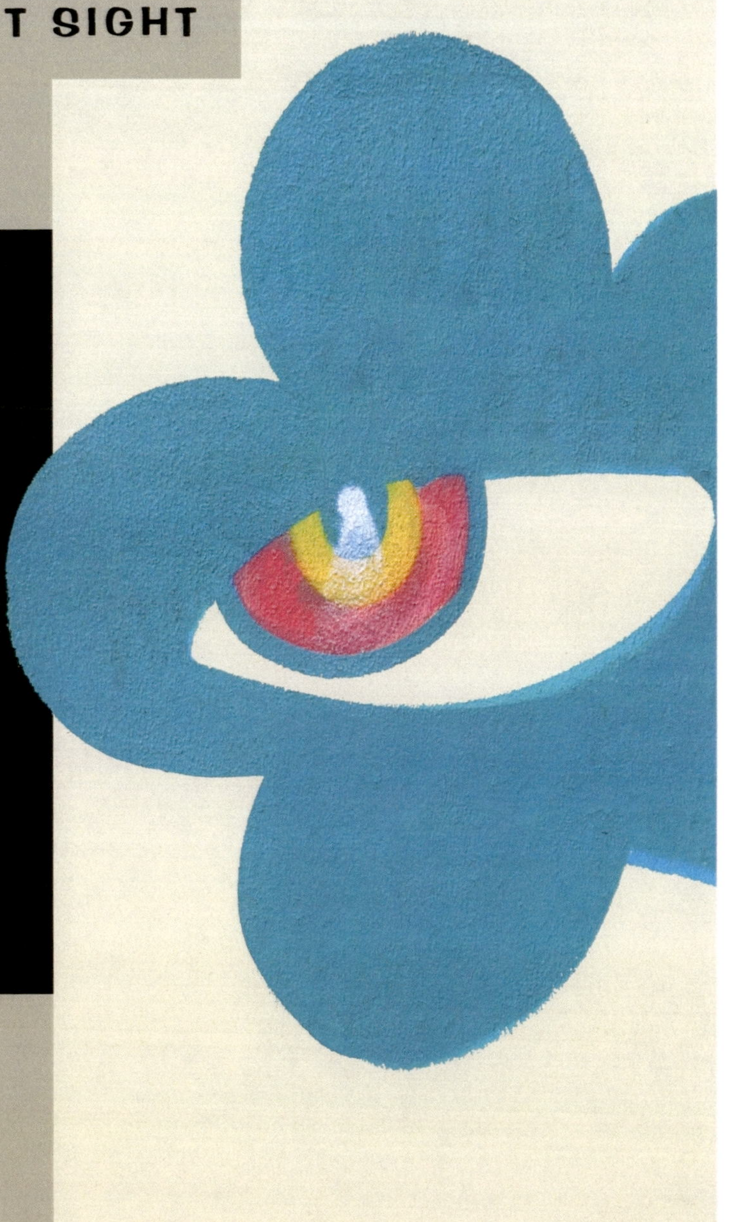

JACOB'S FIRE ESCAPE

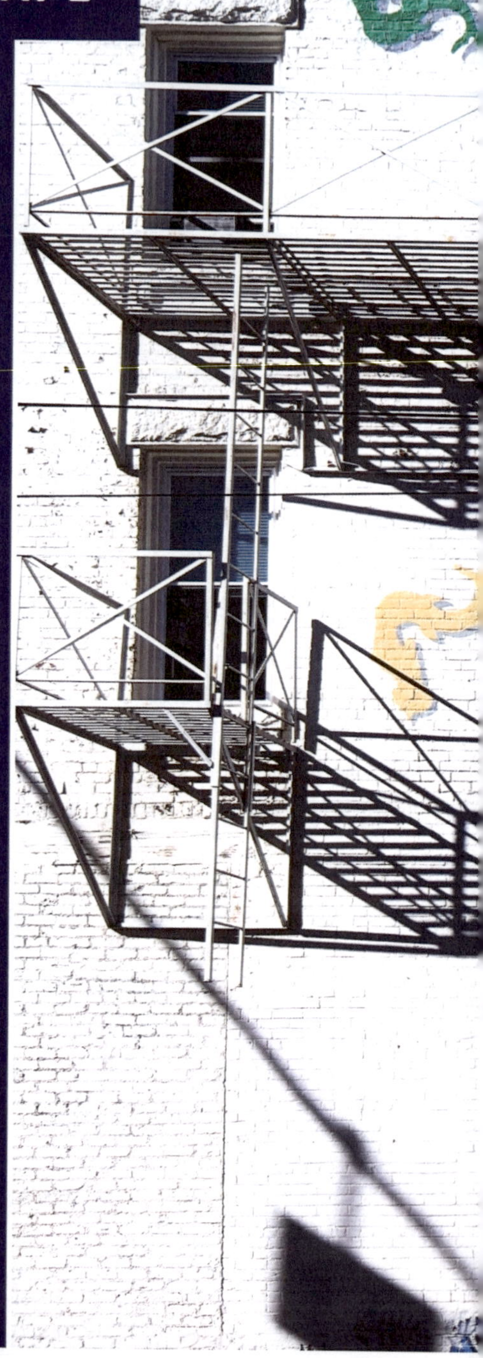

The description appearing in Genesis of
Jacob's dream at Bethel
Beholding a ladder reaching
      From earth to heaven
Is crudely mistranslated, because
Jacob used a stone for a pillow
And the angels of God
Ascending and descending on it
Couldn't have been angels:
Angels have wings, therefore
No need to ascend or descend a ladder
      Or, to clarify, a *fire escape*
I know, because I went out from the day
And went toward night to my bed
And I took a Posturepedic pillow
      And put it under my head
And fell asleep. And I dreamed
And behold, upon the balcony of a fire escape
The Lord cleared away smoke, yelling:
      You need to get the hell out of here
      Before the lake of fire consumes you

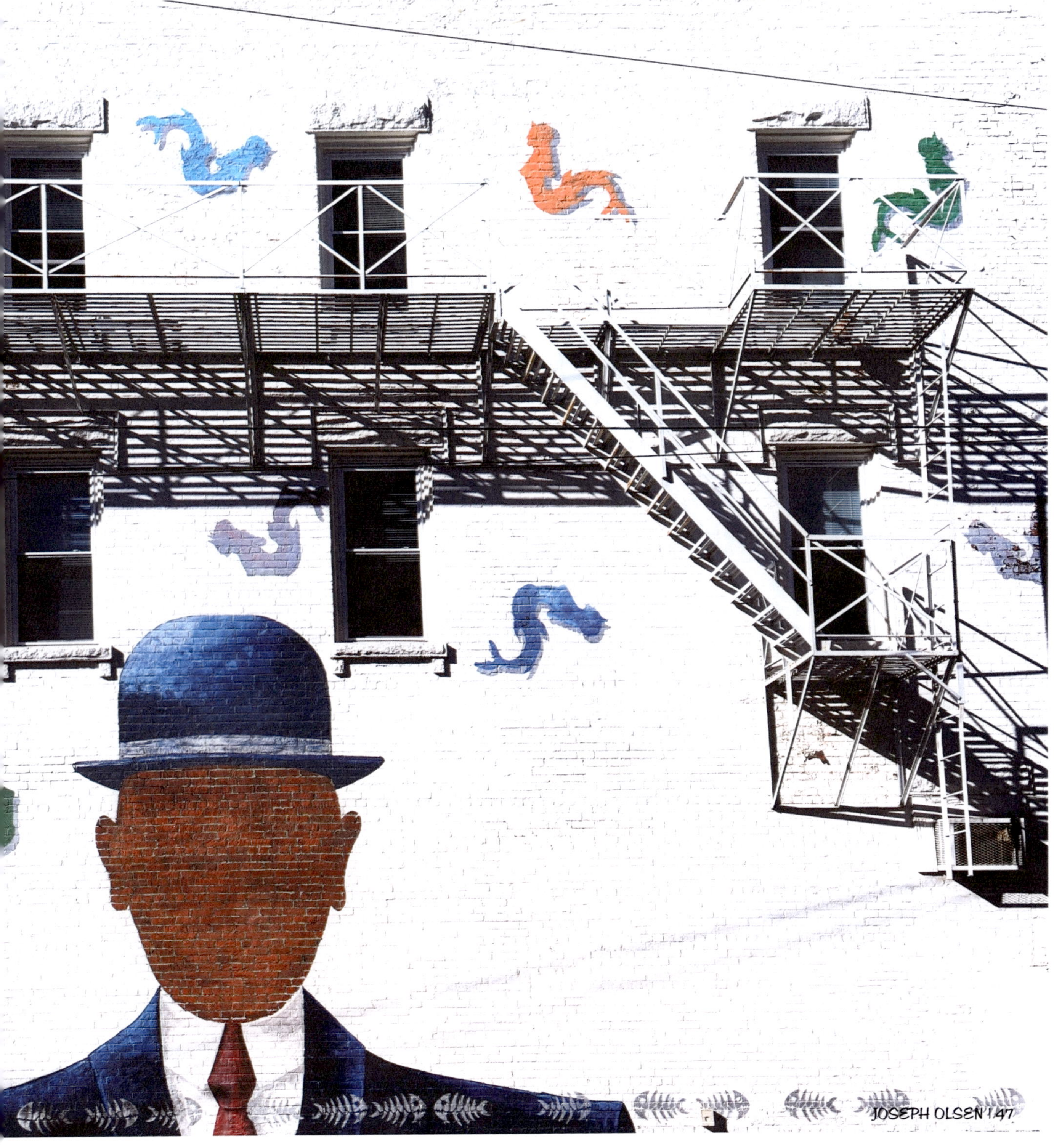
JOSEPH OLSEN '47

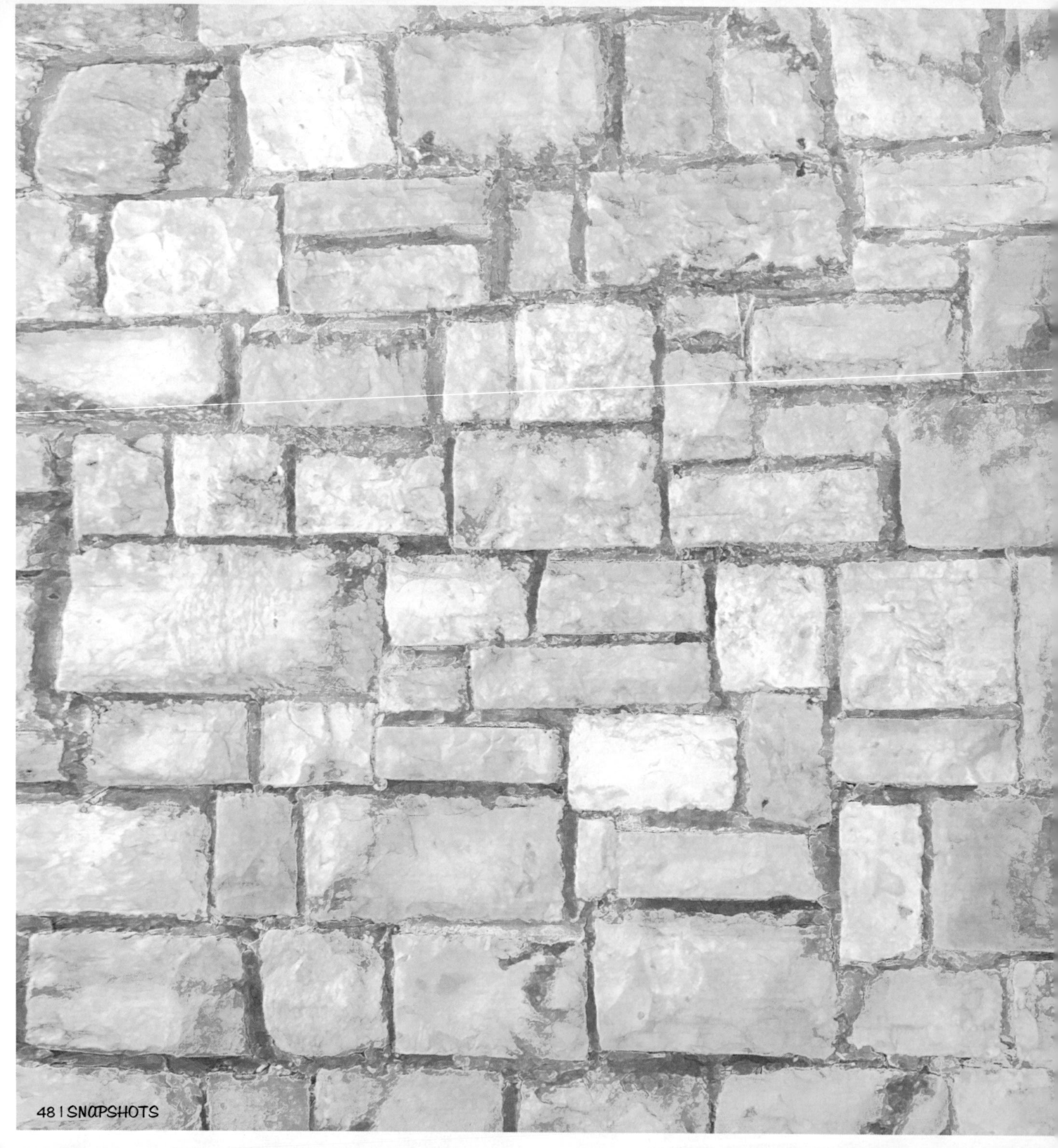

LOOK A LLAMA IN THE EYES

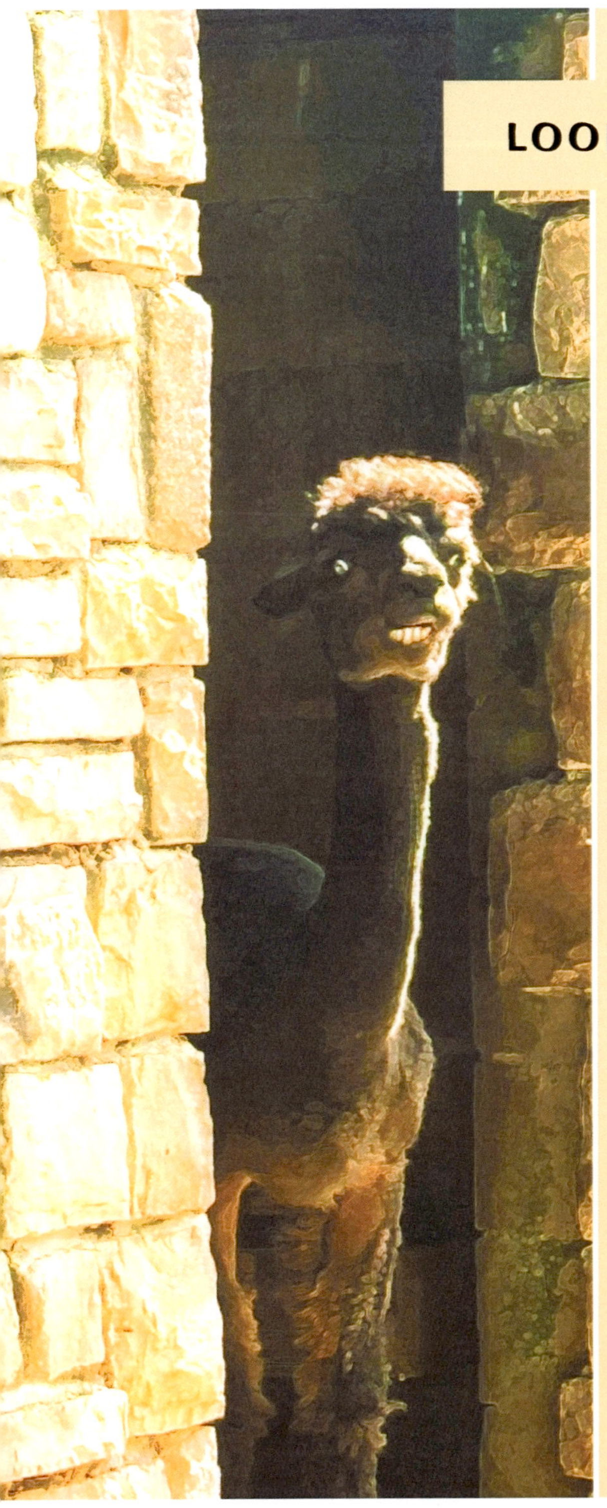

Look a llama in the eyes
And all of you so called *sentient* beings
Too victimized to be a hero
Too vain to notice another
Too technologically advanced to hear
The heart's analog communication of love
Too shallow for deep affection
Too dim-witted to lead a life of meaning
Too proud to admit faults
Too self centered for Christ consciousness
Too ego driven for Buddha nature
Will be seen for who you really are:
Wild God-*damned* animals

20.
Meager possessions
Half naked
In God's favor

21.
You are Technicolor
In a world of
Black and white

22.
My consciousness occupies simultaneous thoughts
Ideas, images, memories and intuitions
This very moment

23.
The light, the sun, the moon, the stars
All good. But Adam and Eve
Ushered out of Eden, not so much

24.
Affirm, Affirm
Affirm - Faithful to this
Pattern of repetition

25.
The box fan
Circulates
Room temperature

THIS VERY MOMENT | IN GOD'S FAVOR

I FLUSHED A URINAL IN MY DREAMS

I flushed a urinal in my dreams
Which represent desires
To cleanse myself of
Negative feelings, toxic thoughts
And unhealthy habits

Now, here in reality
Laid back like a settled baby
Adorned with cute feelings
And nontoxic thoughts
I use a dirty urinal in the mall
Breaking the habit
Of flushing

WHEN WE MAKE IT ACROSS

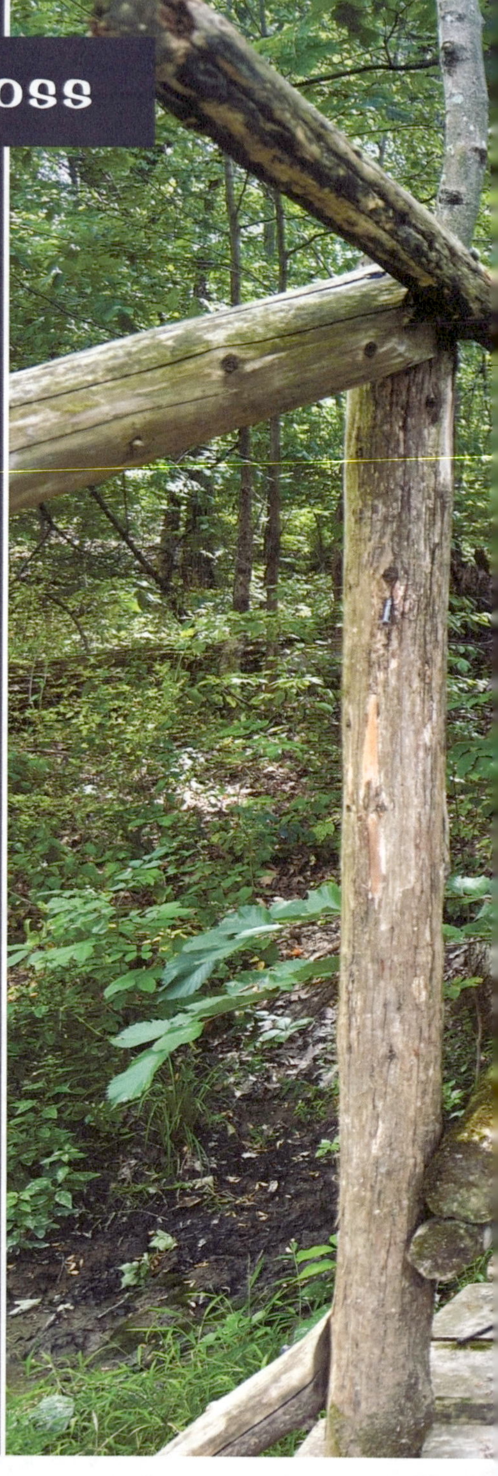

Along the edge of a razor blade
Frightened by touch
       Anxious of
           A promise
              A kiss
                A lie
       Easy, or so it seems
The moments we live for
Are here, above the world
       Heart beating
Along the edge of a razor blade
       Bleeding

On the other side, they sing
       And when we make it across
They will stop briefly to explain
The meaning of our suffering

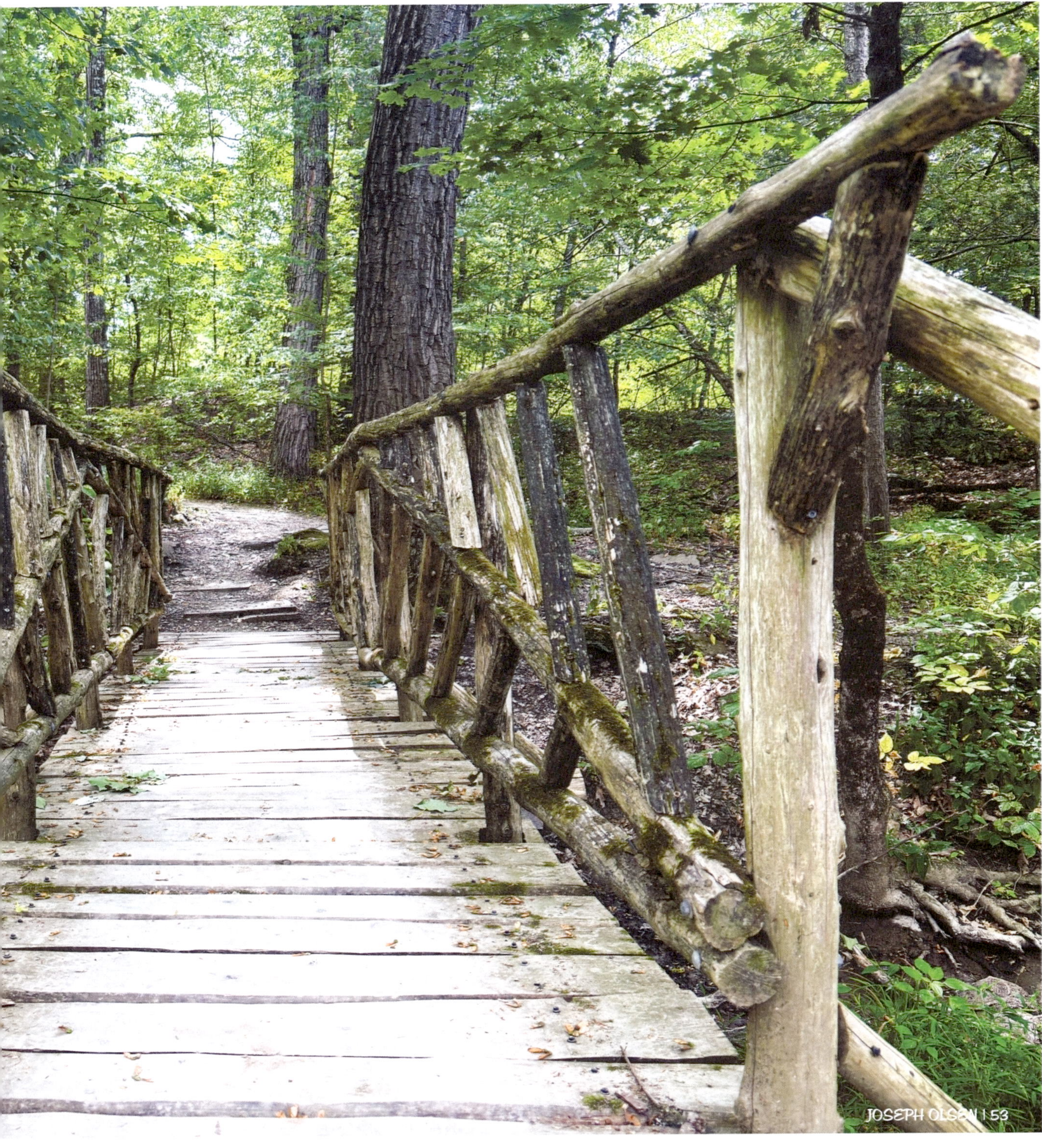
JOSEPH OLSON | 53

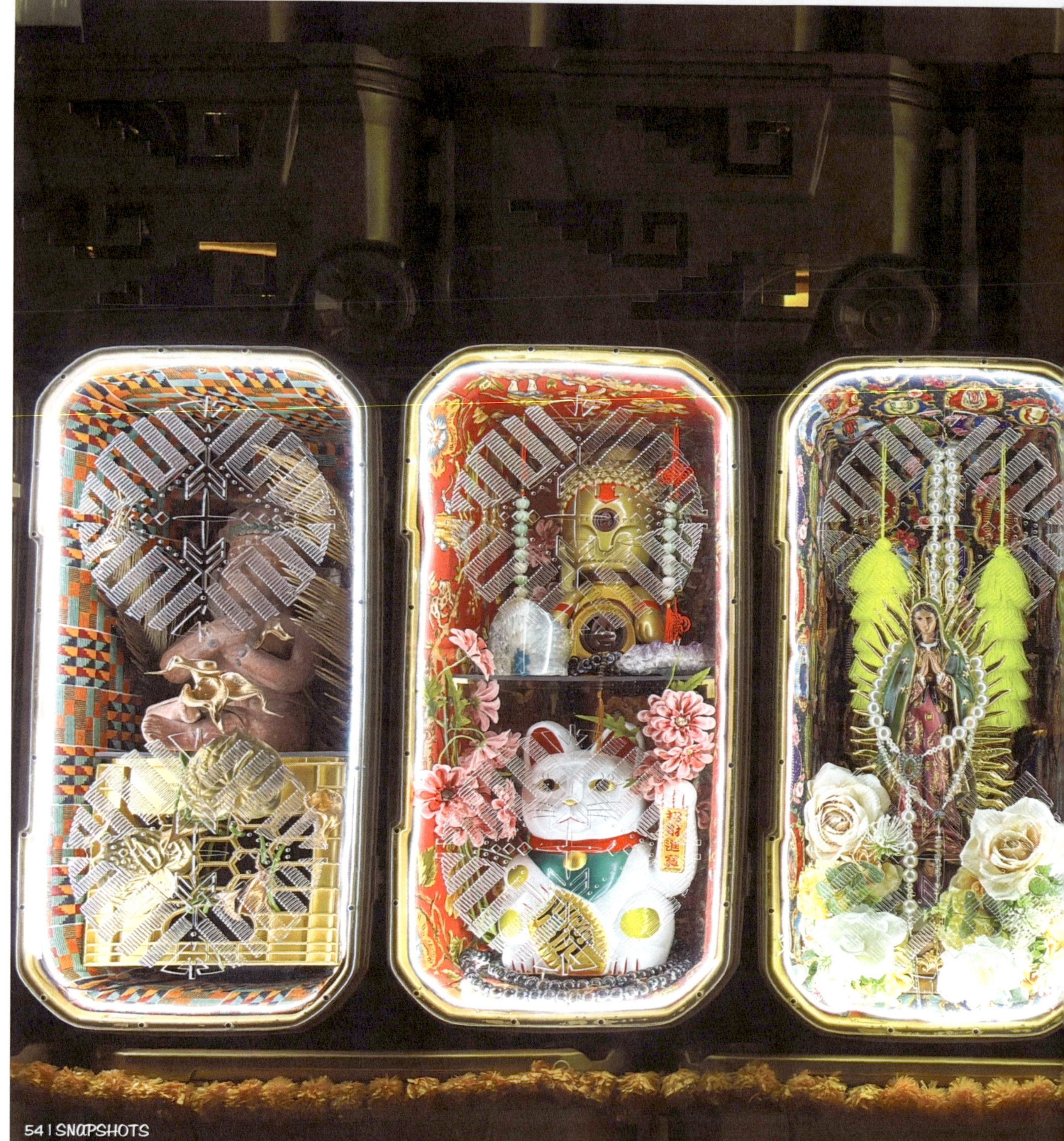

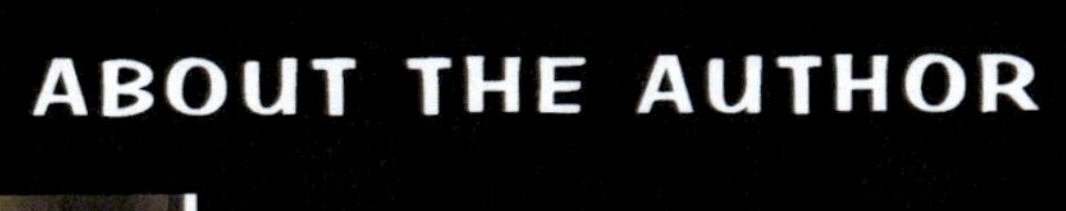

JOSEPH OLSEN

is the author of three books of poetry: *24 Hours*; *Between Us & Imagination*; and this current collection, *Snapshots*.

Olsen was born in the Bronx with nine siblings, but now lives in the Hudson Valley, New York with his wife, Amy, and daughter, Aylin..

INDEX OF PHOTOS

TUNNEL   2 - Rail Trail, New Paltz, NY
CAVE   4 - Rail Trail, Rosendale, NY
PINES   7 - New Windsor, NY
GRAFFITI ALLEY   9 - Chelsea, Manhattan
CHANDELIER   10 - Train Station, Poughkeepsie, NY
EINSTEIN'S FACE ON A WALL   13 - Rail Trail, Highland, NY
ACTION FIGURES   14 - Consignment Shop, Rhinebeck, NY
GRAND CENTRAL TERMINAL   17 - 42nd Street, Manhattan
SHAKESPEARE STATUE   19 - Literary Walk, Central Park, Manhattan
BUILDINGS   19 - Chelsea, Manhattan
HOTEL CHELSEA   21 - West Twenty-Third Street, Manhattan
MANSION TOUR   23 - New York City Public Library, Manhattan
HORSE MANURE   24 - Central Park, Manhattan
CLOUDS   27 - Poet's Walk, Rhinebeck, NY
BEAR   28 - Bounce Arcade, Galleria Mall, Poughkeepsie, NY
WOMAN DANCING   31 - My Town Marketplace, Stone Ridge, NY
STAINED GLASS EMBLEM   32 - Lending library Box at Rec Center, Rosendale, NY
GAMES   35 - Gunks Gaming Guild Cafe, New Paltz, NY
HANDICAPPED LOGO   36 - Tiny Tots Park, Cold Spring, NY
CROWN   36 - Pixabay.com
STORE FRONT   38 - Canada Goose, Fifth Avenue, Manhattan
SUNSET   40 - Cornwall, NY
OAK TREE   42 - Rail Trail, Rosendale, NY
EYE   45 - Underpass, Poughkeepsie, NY
BUILDING PAINTING   47 - North Chestnut Street, Beacon, NY
LLAMA   48 - Forsyth Nature Center, Kingston, NY
URINAL   51 - Restroom, Hudson Valley Mall, Kingston, NY
BRIDGE   53 - Poet's Walk, Rhinebeck, NY
HIGHLINE DISPLAY   54 - Chelsea Highline, Manhattan

BRIDGE/BENCH   Front Cover (Paperback) - Rail Trail, New Paltz, NY
SUNFLOWER   Back Cover (Paperback) - Somebody's front porch, Cold Spring, NY